The Thirty-seven Practices *of* Bodhisattvas

THE THIRTY-SEVEN PRACTICES *of* BODHISATTVAS

An Oral Teaching by

Geshe Sonam Rinchen

Translated and edited by

Ruth Sonam

Snow Lion Publications
Ithaca, New York

Snow Lion Publications
P.O. Box 6483
Ithaca, New York 14851 USA
Tel: 607-273-8519

First edition USA 1997

ISBN 1-55939-068-9

Library of Congress Cataloging-in-Publication Data

Rgyal-sras Thogs-med-dpal Bzaṅ-po-dpal, 1295-1369.
[Rgyal ba'i sras kyi lag len sum cu so bdun ma English]
The thirty seven practices of Bodhisattvas : an oral teaching / by Geshe Sonam Rinchen ; translated and edited by Ruth Sonam.
p. cm.
Includes bibliographical references.
ISBN 1-55939-068-9
1. Enlightenment (Buddhism)--Requisites--Early works to 1800. 2. Spiritual life--Buddhism--Early works to 1800. I. Title.
BQ4399.R4613 1997
294.3'4--dc21 96-37147
CIP

Contents

With gratitude to those, whoever and wherever they may be, who devote themselves to relieving others' suffering. May their courage inspire us to open our hearts.

Acknowledgements

I would like to thank my editor Susan Kyser of Snow Lion Publications and the historian and scholar Tashi Tsering of the Library of Tibetan Works and Archives, Dharamsala, for their assistance.

Introduction

Gyelsay Togmay Sangpo, the author of *The Thirty-seven Practices of Bodhisattvas,* lived from 1295 to 1369. He was born in southwestern Tibet near Sakya. His father was Tosay Künchok Pel and his mother Chaksa Bumdron. They named him Künchok Sangpo. He was an unusual child from the start, but several significant events made him turn to the Buddha's teaching particularly early. His mother died when he was three, after which his father cared for him, but then he also died. From the age of five until he was nine Togmay Sangpo lived with his paternal grandmother. When she died, a maternal uncle took him in and taught him to read and write. At fourteen he became ordained, received the name Sangpo Pel and began to study the three categories of the Buddha's teaching.[1]

Once, when he and his classmates were studying Asanga's *Compendium of Knowledge,*[2] they came across the phrase "suffering without turmoil"[3] and their teacher asked what it meant. Only Togmay Sangpo replied, explaining that it referred to the suffering that a Foe Destroyer, who has rid himself of all the disturbing emotions or turmoil, might experience as a result of past negative actions. His teacher was very pleased with this answer and called him a second Asanga, after which he was always known as "Togmay," the Tibetan for Asanga.

When he was about thirty, he was staying in Ay Monastery[4] near Sakya, studying Mahayana texts on training the mind. By the road behind the monastery lived a destitute man completely covered with lice. Togmay Sangpo used to look after him and bring him food at night. One night the man wasn't in his usual place and though Togmay Sangpo waited, he didn't return. Next morning Togmay searched high and low and eventually found him huddled in a hollow. He asked the man why he had gone there, and the man replied that people were so sickened by his disgusting state, they'd driven him away. Togmay Sangpo was moved to tears. That night he took the man back to his room and fed him till he was satisfied. He then told him to take off his clothes, gave him a clean sheepskin coat along with a few other necessities and sent him on his way.

But now he had the problem of what to do with the old coat full of lice, for if he just threw it away, all the lice would die. Determined to nourish them with his own blood, he put on the coat. Soon he began to look and feel awful and could no longer attend classes. After some days a classmate came to see what had happened and discovered that Togmay was quite ill and depleted. When he reported what he had found to the others, opinions were divided. Some said that he was an admirable practitioner, while others felt it was wrong for a beginner to sacrifice his body in this way. Finally one of them begged him to get rid of the lice for their sake, but he answered that he had lost body after body meaninglessly in past lives, and that this time he meant to make a gift of his body.

After seventeen days, the lice began to die naturally and no new ones were born. He picked out all the dead lice and said mantras over them. Then he ground them up, mixed the powder with clay and made votive tablets out of them. Normally the bones of those we revere and whose kindness we cherish, such as our teachers or parents, are treated in this way. In Tibet sometimes the skulls of animals who had served one faithfully were dried, painted with the six syllable mantra *OM MANI PADME HUNG*[5] and placed on sacred cairns. This was done for the animal's benefit.

From Togmay Sangpo's example we can learn how to turn adverse circumstances into conditions conducive to spiritual development. Once when he was seriously ill, his student Pelden Yeshe asked him what sickness he had and how it could be cured. Togmay Sangpo replied it was the rishis' sickness[6] and that the only thing to do was to pray to the Three Jewels, "If my sickness is of benefit to living beings, may I be sick. If my death would benefit them, may I die, but if my recovery would help, may I be cured. Bless me to accept whatever happens with joy and use it as my path."

When his students pleaded with him to consult doctors and find a cure for their sake, he said, "It's better for this body, which acts as a basis for the 'I,' to be sick. That way bad karma comes to an end. After all, isn't our aim to get rid of the two kinds of obstructions?[7] This will simply hasten the process. If I get well, all the better, for when my body and mind are strong, my virtuous activities will increase, and I can make this human body of mine meaningful. What greater purpose can we have than to create virtue with body, speech and mind?"

On another occasion he said, "If I don't have wealth, there's less for me to hoard and protect, and I won't be involved in quarrels, conflicts or disputes which often arise over material possessions. But if I become wealthy, all the better, for I can use what I have to make offerings to the Three Jewels and gifts to the poor. This will increase my positive energy, the source of all temporary and ultimate well-being."

He also said, "If I die soon, that's fine because negative conditions that could prevent the awakening of good imprints won't have time to arise. If I live long, that's fine too because the seeds for insights, which lie dormant in me, will be nurtured by the instructions of my teachers. Through long and concerted practice these insights will arise, just as a seed that comes in contact with nurturing warmth and moisture eventually sprouts. Then I'll harvest the fruit!"

By thinking like him, we can turn our body into a city of joy. It is possible—Togmay Sangpo did it. He knew how to transform what others see as suffering into a source of happiness. He practised this himself and handed on the secret. Even if we're unable to follow his instructions at present, we can make fervent wishes to do so in future and create much positive energy just through this.

When he was sick, he understood that his sickness had no objective existence and saw in it a reminder of the infallible connection between actions and their effects—that positive actions bring agreeable results and negative actions disagreeable ones. Using his sickness, he contemplated how things appear though they are empty and are empty but appear. He accepted sickness as part of cyclic existence and let it remind him to develop the patience which willingly accepts hardship. For him it became a means of purifying negativities and obstructions and a source of greater compassion for other living beings. It's said that Togmay Sangpo's profound serenity even affected his cat to such an extent that it lost all interest in hunting mice and turned vegetarian.

When it became clear that his death was imminent, his student Pel Yewa asked him where he would be reborn. Togmay Sangpo answered, "Geshe Langritangpa[8] prayed to be reborn in the hells. I, too, would willingly take rebirth there, if it were of benefit to living beings. I don't want to be reborn in a pure land,[9] if that isn't of use to others, but I have no control over these matters. All I can do is request the Three Jewels to give me a body which will be useful to others."

The first Dalai Lama, Gyelwa Gendün Drup[10] was asked in which pure land he intended to take birth. He answered, "How can I leave suffering living beings here and go to a pure land?" And indeed, he has remained with us in the world. Geshe Chekawa,[11] whose whole life was devoted to the cultivation of the altruistic intention to attain enlightenment for the sake of all living beings and to the ideal of helping others, instructed his attendants to set up offerings when he was dying, telling them that things were not working out as he'd planned. Concerned, they asked what was wrong and whether they could do anything. He replied, "I've been praying to take rebirth in the hells so as to help others, but I keep having visions of pure lands." If we want to be reborn in a pure land, the surest way is to cultivate a kind heart. Without that, our road to the pure lands is blocked.

As Longdöl Lama Rinpoche's[12] death was approaching, he said, "This morning I have an old man's body, but by evening I'll have the youthful body of a celestial being." He could die without grief or fear because his heart was full of the teachings, and he was free from regrets and guilt.

Prologue

Togmay Sangpo's work is about training the mind. What does that entail? Ideally, it means ridding ourselves completely of all disturbing emotions and their imprints, but at the very least it should help us to prevent their coarser forms and gradually to decrease them. The text is called *The Thirty-seven Practices of Bodhisattvas.*[13] It consists of forty-three verses, of which the first two are an expression of homage and a commitment to write the text. This is followed by thirty-seven verses of advice to the beginner on how to practise. There are four concluding verses.

Homage to Lokeshwara

The author begins the text with a brief homage, merely mentioning Chenrezig's[14] name in Sanskrit. It is followed by a more extensive homage to the spiritual teacher inseparable from Chenrezig, the embodiment of enlightened compassion.

I pay constant homage through my three doors,
To my supreme teacher and protector Chenrezig,
Who while seeing all phenomena lack coming and going,
Makes single-minded effort for the good of living beings.

The text deals with the two kinds of altruistic intention, the main focus of practice here: the conventional altruistic intention which is concerned entirely with others' good, and the ultimate altruistic intention which knows reality as it is. To develop these we need compassion. The growth of both compassion and the altruistic intention depends upon the spiritual teacher inseparable from Chenrezig, who in a causal capacity inspires and blesses us to develop them. The spiritual teacher inseparable from Chenrezig is also the result of cultivating the two kinds of altruistic intention, in that we ourselves come to embody the qualities he possesses.

What does this indicate to those who aspire to practise the teachings? If we wish to cherish others and understand reality, we must cultivate compassion ourselves and seek the blessings, inspiration, instruction and support of our spiritual teacher inseparable from Chenrezig.

The homage here is paid through praise. "All phenomena" refers to everything that exists—the aggregates, sources and constituents,[15] both things as they are in their fundamental nature and in all their diversity, contaminated and uncontaminated. These categories include all phenomena. Everything is free from inherent coming and going, free from the extremes of permanence and annihilation, free from inherent production and cessation and free from being inherently one or many. These eight features are described at the beginning of Nagarjuna's *Treatise on the Middle Way*.[16]

The fundamental nature of things is free from all fabrications of true existence. Meditating on this fundamental nature pacifies all conventional appearances, in the sense that they are absent when reality is perceived directly. Eventually this also pacifies all our conceptions of true existence and their imprints. The spiritual teacher in the form of Chenrezig is praised for his direct perception of the fundamental nature of all phenomena.

The breadth and depth of the ocean of cyclic existence is unfathomable. Living beings are drowning in it, attacked from all sides by the crocodiles and sea monsters of the three poisons and other disturbing emotions. These torment us daily and never give us a moment's respite. Isn't it true that we're almost always experiencing some kind of trouble or pain? In Australia someone told me that a man went fishing and was attacked by a crocodile which devoured him, while a bystander filmed the whole thing. I was horrified. This was a story about a single crocodile, but we're constantly attacked by many! The depth and breadth of a normal ocean can be measured, but the ocean of cyclic existence is limitless. The false view of the transitory collection[17] as a real "I" and "mine" is compared to a net in which we're ensnared. We can move around a little inside it but cannot escape. This constricting net of conceptions is our prison.

Though Chenrezig sees the true nature of things, he is moved by compassion for living beings. At the beginning of his *Supplement to the Middle Way*[18] Chandrakirti pays homage to three kinds of compassion: that which focuses on living beings, on phenomena and on the unobservable.[19] Here Chenrezig is praised for the latter kind of compassion, which is supported by an understanding of reality. He keeps constant watch over living beings, always ready to reach them the helping hands of love and compassion. We sometimes act prematurely, sometimes too late, but Chenrezig is ready to act at just the right moment. The trouble is we turn away!

The text says "to my supreme teacher," which may be taken to refer to Togmay Sangpo's personal teacher, while "protector Chenrezig" refers to Chenrezig as spiritual teacher to all beings of the three worlds.[20]

Perfect Buddhas, source of all well-being and happiness,
Arise from accomplishing the excellent teachings,
And this depends on knowing the practices.
So I will explain the practices of Bodhisattvas.

This is the author's commitment to write the text. Our own and others' temporary and ultimate well-being, the object of our aspirations, comes about through perfect Buddhas. How?

Happiness depends on properly cultivating what is wholesome and discarding what is unwholesome. Those who show us exactly how to do this are enlightened beings. They do it through their teaching which arises from the exalted wisdom of their enlightened mind.

Enlightened activity[21] may be considered from the point of view of both the subject and the object. It originates from enlightened beings and is experienced by us. Each positive thought we have is said to be the result of enlightened activity, arising from the wisdom of a Buddha. Shantideva[22] says:

> A flash of lightning on a dark cloudy night
> Illuminates things for just an instant.
> Similarly, through the Buddha's power
> Occasionally a good thought briefly arises.

On a dark cloudy night a flash of lightning illuminates everything for just a moment and then all is darkness again. Through the power of a Buddha's enlightened activity, every once in a while we have a wholesome thought or feeling, but usually this is as short-lived as a flash of lightning. Such thoughts are sporadic and weak, arise with difficulty, do not last long and are incomplete in that we cannot sustain their virtuous momentum from the beginning to the end of an action. Unwholesome thoughts and feelings are spontaneous, sustained and complete in every way. They're like the thick cloud cover during a long dark night. Since they produce intense suffering, we must try to cultivate virtue and avoid non-virtue.

Enlightened beings are our ultimate refuge and our ultimate goal, for we ourselves seek enlightenment. From them come the excellent teachings which instruct us in how to practise. We must hear and think about the scriptural teachings[23] in order to embody them by gaining insights.[24] This ocean of teachings is vast and a beginner cannot know them all. The author promises to render their essence concisely according to the scriptures. Often things sound easy when we hear them, but afterwards we find it difficult to recall exactly what was said.

1 The Good Ship

The thirty-seven verses which form the main part of the text explain the causes for the altruistic intention, the altruistic intention itself and the precepts of training. The altruistic intention arises from compassion which is strong enough to induce the special wish to take personal responsibility for the welfare of living beings. This compassion is the inability to bear the suffering of living beings as limitless as space and the intense wish to free them from it.

First we must recognize our own suffering and fully understand how contaminated actions and disturbing emotions imprison us in cyclic existence. When we feel a strong aversion to our own condition and desire liberation, we will easily empathize with others in the same situation and feel genuine compassion for them. To develop such a wish for liberation we must begin by appreciating the preciousness of our human life.

1 **Having gained this rare ship of freedom and fortune,**
Hear, think and meditate unwaveringly night and day
In order to free yourself and others
From the ocean of cyclic existence—
This is the practice of Bodhisattvas.

Freedom refers to our freedom from eight adverse conditions. Four of these are non-human states in which there is no opportunity for spiritual practice. Hell-beings are tormented by extreme heat or cold, hungry ghosts by hunger and thirst. Animals are limited by their lack of intelligence and are constantly in fear of being attacked and devoured. The suffering of these beings is so intense that they cannot begin to think about spiritual practice. Celestial beings with long lives are absorbed in sensual pleasures or the pleasure of concentration and cannot develop an aversion to cyclic existence. Their bodies and minds are not suitable as a basis for vows of any kind.

There are four human states which prevent spiritual practice, the most serious of which is holding wrong views. Belief that there are no past and future lives and that there is no connection between actions and their effects severs the continuity of past virtue and makes the creation of fresh virtue impossible.

Being born a barbarian in a remote place, where there is no access to Buddhist teachings and there are no followers of the Buddha, is also an insurmountable impediment. Local customs and the habitual way of life would probably conflict with the spirit of the teachings, and we would never even hear of them. We also cannot practise if we're born at a time when a Buddha's teachings do not exist in the world. Defective faculties, particularly defective mental faculties, are a severe limitation. Even blindness or deafness makes ordinary daily life extremely difficult. If our mental state does not allow us to differentiate between right and wrong, how can we engage in spiritual practice?

Fortune means enjoying conducive conditions. Five kinds of such fortune are personal: being born as a human; being born in a place where the teachings exist and there are ordained men and women; possessing healthy faculties; not having created any seriously negative actions like the five extremely grave and the five almost as grave actions;[25]

having faith in spiritual teachers, the three kinds of training and the texts which contain instructions on them. Five kinds of good fortune are circumstantial: that a Buddha has come to the world; that he has lit the lamp of the teachings; that these teachings are alive insofar as there are people who hear, think about and meditate on them; that there are those who can be looked upon as role-models because of their exemplary practice of the teachings; and that support and encouragement for practitioners is available.

We must consider whether we enjoy all eighteen of these freedoms and riches. This human life is our ship. With it we can ferry ourselves and others across the sea of cyclic existence, which makes it very precious and important. We are the captain, this body and mind are our vessel. If you have a rich cargo, you need a stalwart and seaworthy ship. The cargo is our store of merit and insight, the crew our fellow practitioners. We're bound for the port of liberation.

A rich human life of this kind is precious but rare. We will appreciate its rarity if we consider the causes needed to create it, the factors which constitute it and its scarcity as illustrated by examples.[26] Not only is it precious and rare but very vulnerable. Therefore we must not waste this precious opportunity, but should, without distraction, practise day and night, sleeping only in the middle part of the night. How are we to practise? By hearing, thinking and meditating on the true meaning of the teachings.

2 Leaving Home

Someone intent on making best use of their human life and attaining liberation by extracting the very essence of the teachings must avoid bad places and everything which arouses disturbing emotions, for as beginners we lack familiarity with the antidotes used to counteract them. Sufficient training and familiarity will insure the constant presence of non-attachment, restraint from anger and a lack of confusion, but at present the poisonous emotions still arise automatically as soon as we encounter conditions that stimulate them.

2 **Attached to your loved ones you're stirred up like water.**
Hating your enemies you burn like fire.
In the darkness of confusion you forget what to adopt and discard.
Give up your homeland—
This is the practice of Bodhisattvas.

If we aspire to attain enlightenment for others, we must give up worldly concerns and concentrate on practising purely. To do this we may need to leave our home and country, which are often a source of disturbing emotions. Ordinary people generally consider their country as the dearest, most beautiful and best place in the world, but for practising the teachings it may easily be the worst because our way of life there often conflicts with the teachings, while circumstances which prevent pure practice abound.

From birth we're surrounded by our parents, siblings and relations. Later we acquire partners and children. The affection we feel for them is mixed with possessiveness. Attachment to our own, to friends and to sensual pleasures sweeps over us like waves and stirs us up like turbulent water. We find all of them difficult to give up.

Those who harm us or the places and property we own and those who oppose us or do not share our ideology are conventionally viewed as enemies. Their conduct seems intentional and we feel hostile towards them. Anger blazes in us like the flames that flare up when firewood soaked in oil is set alight. Our so-called friends and enemies keep us busy and preoccupied. The customs and habits associated with our normal way of life at home arouse strong emotions and create many distractions. We forget what really is worth doing and what isn't.

We think of a place with wild flowers, meadows, forests, clean water and wildlife, where we feel like taking off our shoes and running barefoot, as a good place. But if it gives rise to clinging attachment or animosity, it's a bad place for us. These are external factors which can prevent us from practising purely.

3 By avoiding bad objects, disturbing emotions gradually decrease.
Without distraction, virtuous activities naturally increase.
With clarity of mind, conviction in the teaching arises.
Cultivate seclusion—
This is the practice of Bodhisattvas.

Disturbing emotions and their seeds don't just vanish when we avoid the objects which stimulate them, but we can prevent them from arising by making the causes which trigger them as incomplete as possible and by trying to give up the eight worldly concerns.[27] At the same time we continuously cultivate the antidotes which counteract and eventually uproot the disturbing emotions. Unwholesome activity induced by the disturbing emotions then decreases, and we're able to observe ethical discipline. Our lives become less busy: there's less activity, not so many visitors and no need to make quite so many cups of tea and coffee or wonder what to cook for dinner.

In Tibet guests weren't a problem. The tea was always hot and there was tsampa, flour made from roasted barley, in a wooden box—butter and cheese as well, if the family was reasonably well off. There was no need to wash up, as all guests had their own wooden bowl, used only by them, tucked into the loose front of their chuba.[28] Tibetans must all have been excellent practitioners because of their simple lifestyle! In the monasteries, to save time, some monks didn't light a fire to make tea but mixed cold water with their tsampa,[29] set it aside for a short while and then ate it.

Less busyness allows us to put more energy into refining our physical, verbal and mental activities. Our interest in ordinary time-consuming pursuits decreases, our clinging attachment and anger subside and by gradually ridding ourselves of slackness and excitement in meditation, we gain the ability to maintain single-pointed concentration. As our body and mind become serviceable, our mental clarity increases. This leads to greater conviction regarding what should be cultivated and what should be discarded. The benefit of remaining in seclusion is that our practice of the three kinds of training—in ethical discipline, concentration and wisdom—grows as described.

It's not worth investing so much energy in worldly matters. Everyone has a different disposition, different interests and capacities. Buddhas perceive all these individual idiosyncracies clearly and can perform enlightened actions of every kind, yet even they cannot please everyone. We lack such insight and the scope of our actions is extremely limited, so how can we hope to gain everyone's approval? If we live simply without wealth or fame, others pity and criticize us. If we get rich and famous, they say what we own must have been acquired dishonestly. It's hard to get on with other people and much easier to get on with meadows, forests and wild animals, so why not seek a quiet, secluded place?

3 Letting Go

So far the author has made us aware of the preciousness of our human life and the need to use it to practise the teachings. He advises us to avoid situations which could prevent us from doing this and recommends that we seek seclusion. But there's little point in isolating ourselves from physical busyness, if all we're concerned with is this life. We may go into retreat, put up a big notice outside our cave: "No visitors. Retreat in progress" and then sit inside wondering what other people think of us. That means we're still caught up with worldly concerns.

It's necessary to keep an alert watch over the three doors and to seclude not only the body but also the mind from busyness. As long as we remain engrossed in this life, we're not even genuine practitioners of the Buddha's teaching. Normally we invest much energy in trying to secure rewards, a good reputation and a circle of friends, but it's not certain that we'll acquire what we seek. Even if we succeed, we may not have the opportunity to enjoy the fruits of our efforts. When death comes, as it certainly will, we must relinquish everything for which we've striven. Since all these things are essenceless, we must try to overcome our preoccupation with them by remembering how difficult it is to attain a human life of freedom and fortune, how precious it is and how impermanent.

Once we recognize that the so-called good things of life are unreliable and essenceless, we'll begin to think about what happens after death. Either rebirth in a state of suffering or as a human or celestial being lies ahead. By taking sincere refuge and acting in accordance with the connection between actions and their effects, we can insure a good rebirth. This requires giving up all forms of violence and doing what we can to help others, a way of life which will bring us happiness now and in the future.

Restraint from violence towards others is ultimately a way of protecting ourselves, for whatever harms others indirectly harms us too. Non-violence doesn't simply mean not doing certain things. It is conscious and active restraint in the form of seven physical and verbal virtues[30] based on non-attachment, freedom from anger and freedom from confusion. Gradually we cultivate non-attachment towards the concerns of this life, towards cyclic existence in general and towards just our own personal happiness. Freedom from anger means actively developing love and compassion based on a wish to help others. But we must know how and this entails overcoming ignorance, especially concerning the nature of reality.

Thinking about the preciousness and impermanence of our human existence is a way to counter compulsive attachment to matters of this life. We're told to "give up this life" but that isn't an instruction to destroy ourselves or give away everything we own. It means giving up the clinging attachment we feel towards our body and possessions because too much preoccupation with them leaves us little time and energy for spiritual practice. Of course, many ordinary things give us pleasure and happiness, but the satisfaction we gain is rather like that derived from scratching an itchy sore—very short-lived. How much better to be rid of the sore!

Often our brief pleasures turn into pain. Lasting happiness can only be gained by cutting through craving and the ignorance which underlies it. This can't be done quickly, but in the meantime we can insure that we don't find ourselves in a worse situation than at present. It's wise to sacrifice small pleasures for lasting happiness and bear some hardship in order to free ourselves from suffering.

4 Loved ones who have long kept company will part.
Wealth created with difficulty will be left behind.
Consciousness, the guest, will leave the guest-house of the body.
Let go of this life—
This is the practice of Bodhisattvas.

Throughout our beginningless time in cyclic existence every living being has been in different relationships to us. Sometimes they've been friends, sometimes enemies, but there isn't one with whom we haven't had a relationship. This raises a lot of important questions: what is cyclic existence? Why is it beginningless? Can something which isn't a living being ever become one? If not, it makes sense that we've been in every kind of relationship with every being. This is a vast topic and deals with fundamental Buddhist beliefs which are not just based on scriptural citations but can be substantiated by reasoning.

From the second moment of a relationship separation has already begun. Separation from all those we love—parents, siblings, partners, children, friends and spiritual teachers—is inevitable. We expect relationships to last and see both friends and enemies as fixed in their roles, which leads to strong attachment or animosity towards them. But everything that meets must part. If we can remind ourselves of this and stay aware of it, we won't be so shocked when the separation occurs. This doesn't mean we should avoid relationships or cultivate indifference. On the contrary, since separation is unavoidable, we must make the brief time we spend together meaningful and valuable and do as much as we can to help each other, so that we have nothing to regret.

We're ready to perform negative actions, undergo hardship and spare no effort to acquire homes, cars and other possessions, but in the end we must leave them behind. We can take nothing and nothing can follow us when we die. We don't need to give up our property now, but if we overcome our clinging attachment to it, we'll not suffer later when death forces us to part from what we own. Togmay Sangpo was quite happy to have possessions. He said they would allow him to create much positive energy by helping others, which in the long run brings happiness. It's also fine to have a circle of loving and helpful friends, for we can do much good helping each other.

This body is like a guest-house and our consciousness like a traveller on the roads of worldly existence. A traveller keeps moving on from one hotel to another and cannot remain in the same one forever. We must definitely part from friends, possessions and our body. We don't know where our friends are going nor for what rebirth we're bound. Only our consciousness, bearing the imprints of our positive and negative actions, and the "I" attributed to it will go on to the next life. The kind of rebirth we take depends on whether positive or negative imprints predominate and which are activated when we die.

The less we cling and the more we wish to help, the more peaceful our physical and verbal actions become. This influences others and makes their minds more peaceful too, which in turn affects their actions. Rubbing two rough surfaces together will not make them smooth, but by rubbing a rough surface and a smooth one together, the rough one gradually becomes smooth. There are so many unruly living beings, we cannot hope to subdue them all. The only thing to do is to subdue our own mind. No one ever leaves this world having put down all their detractors.

5 **When you keep their company your three poisons increase,**
Your activities of hearing, thinking and meditating decline,
And they make you lose your love and compassion.
Give up bad friends—
This is the practice of Bodhisattvas.

No matter how hard we're trying to practise, what we do will be undermined if we keep bad company. Bad friends aren't instantly recognizable because they don't have horns or cloven hooves. They may be affectionate, helpful and well-meaning people, but through their influence our previous virtue declines, we get involved in unwholesome physical, verbal and mental activity and stop creating fresh virtue. Our disturbing emotions increase and we feel disinclined to hear, think or meditate. Unintentionally we get drawn into their busyness and unedifying conversations. We feel less interested in the idea of liberation. Our loving wish to bring others happiness, our compassionate wish to free them from suffering and our altruistic intention all grow weaker. This may happen as the result of our parents' or teachers' influence, in which case even they count as bad friends. In the long run such negative influence is detrimental to our reputation and standing in this life and to the virtue which leads to eventual liberation.

This is not hard to understand but important because it affects our life-style and the kind of relationships we form. The advice to give up bad friends doesn't involve disliking them. These are Mahayana instructions, and a fundamental Mahayana precept is not to abandon any living being. However, since we're beginners, it may entail living at a distance from those who have an adverse influence on us.

4 Trusting

6 **When you rely on them your faults come to an end**
And your good qualities grow like the waxing moon.
Cherish spiritual teachers
Even more than your own body—
This is the practice of Bodhisattvas.

Who are our good friends? When we're setting out on the journey through unknown territory to liberation and enlightenment, we need a guide. Both the Lesser Vehicle and the Great Vehicle, sutra and tantra alike, stress the importance of cultivating a relationship with a spiritual teacher. A spiritual teacher is a good friend. The qualities required of the teacher and student vary according to the different systems, but it's always emphasized that the student should have faith, respect and the wish to please the spiritual teacher through his or her actions.

No matter to what culture we belong, the advice to avoid bad friends and keep the company of good ones is universal. Our parents give us this advice and so does the Buddha, for the good reason that the company we keep has a profound effect on us. The influence of good friends will help us get rid of physical, verbal and mental faults and overcome hindrances to the three kinds of training. Our coarse, uncouth and unwholesome physical behaviour will decrease and our speech will become less rough and hurtful.

All good qualities leading to high status, namely a rebirth as a celestial or human being, and to definite goodness, which is liberation from cyclic existence, will increase. The main causes for high status and definite goodness are faith and wisdom respectively. Under the influence of a good spiritual friend these will grow like the waxing moon.

What kind of spiritual teacher should we seek? The peacock-like spiritual teacher is best. Peacocks look rather plain and lumpy from a distance, but when we get close we discover the irridescent beauty of their glorious feathers. Maitreya's *Ornament for the Mahayana Sutras* describes ten qualities possessed by the ideal spiritual teacher.[31] In the fifth chapter of *Engaging in the Bodhisattva Deeds* Shantideva also speaks of the spiritual teacher's qualities:

> Never, even at the cost of your life,
> Give up a spiritual teacher who
> Is versed in the meaning of the Great Vehicle
> And lives by the supreme discipline of Bodhisattvas.

Even if the Buddha appeared in person, he would probably seem quite ordinary to us because of our present predispositions. Whether or not our teacher is famous, powerful or clairvoyant is unimportant. Of course, thinking our teacher is clairvoyant may have a salutary effect, but the vision and knowledge of Buddhas and Bodhisattvas is unimpeded, and we are, in any case, constantly under their watchful eye. An affinity between our own and our teacher's disposition and interests is important, if we want the relationship to last. Our spiritual teacher should not only possess a good knowledge of what must be cultivated and discarded but be able to explain it correctly. He or she should be compassionate and motivated by a genuine wish to help. For us such a teacher is the embodiment of all the Conquerors and their children. Even a Buddha cannot wash away our wrong-doing, remove our suffering with his hands or give us his realizations. But he can teach us about the four noble truths without any distortion, and if we practise according to his instructions, we can gain freedom.

Trust and confidence are vital. If we don't trust the teacher, we won't have confidence in the instructions we're given and will not put them into practice. Knowledge, kindness and good ethics are essential. The teacher can't be expected to know everything, but he or she should possess the knowledge we're seeking. Kindness doesn't mean cloying, honey-like sweetness. Out of kindness our teacher may be quite firm or even stern with us. Good ethics makes the spiritual teacher's company pleasing. If we wish to take vows, our teacher should hold them, know how to bestow them, be able to explain how we must hold them, what constitute transgressions and what is done to purify them. Even in a secular context a good teacher needs ample knowledge of the subject and should be capable of establishing a good rapport with the student. A poor relationship is not conducive to learning.

When we find a good teacher, we should cherish him or her more than our body and life, which we love above all else. We must try to please the spiritual teacher through our physical, verbal and mental activity, by making gifts, offering our services and, most importantly, by practising what he or she instructs. Good qualities result from cultivating the relationship with our spiritual teacher in the proper way.

In the *Great Exposition of the Stages of the Path*[32] Tsongkhapa speaks at length about this relationship. He tells us that if we're seeking a spiritual teacher or ever intend to act as one, we must know what qualities are required. We must also know what qualities the student should possess, of which the most important are open-mindedness, intelligence and enthusiastic interest.

If a spiritual teacher, who possesses many excellent qualities, agrees to take care of us, we must use the opportunity to cross the ocean of cyclic existence. We now need a suitable refuge to help us gain freedom from the fears of worldly existence and solitary peace.

7 **Bound himself in the jail of cyclic existence,**
What worldly god can give you protection?
Therefore when you seek refuge, take refuge in
The Three Jewels which will not betray you—
This is the practice of Bodhisattvas.

There are many well-known powerful worldly gods and forces which, because they're still controlled by contaminated actions and disturbing emotions, remain like ourselves within the prison of cyclic existence. Influenced by sources of suffering like the three poisons, they perform harmful actions which express their hostility and desire. The praises extolling such worldly gods actually laud them for these very activities. From a Buddhist point of view, this shows they're still trapped within cyclic existence and therefore, no matter how powerful, are incapable of protecting others from suffering and fear. If you're sinking in a swamp yourself, you're not in a position to rescue anyone else. In order to be fully capable of showing others how to free themselves, you must be free from cyclic existence yourself. We need a refuge we can trust and which will not let us down. The Three Jewels are such a refuge, for they will never fail us. Taking refuge in them, we look upon the enlightened beings as those who show us our true protection. We regard their teaching as our actual refuge and the spiritual community as our companions and role-models. When we are overwhelmed by obstructions, feel afraid or are in pain, we have a support and a source of strength and hope. Feeling this trust is taking mental refuge, expressing it in words is taking verbal refuge and making any gesture of homage is taking physical refuge. We then try to live by the refuge precepts.[33]

When we see no way out, when we look to our right and left but no one, not even enlightened beings and our spiritual teachers, can do anything directly to help us, there's no need for despair because the virtue we ourselves have created will act as our refuge and protection.

If we imagine our spiritual teachers and the Three Jewels before us, thinking again and again of their excellent qualities, we'll remember them not only during our waking hours but during the night as well. Through such prolonged familiarity we will, hopefully, also recall them when we're dying.

5 Commitment

8 **The Subduer said all the unbearable suffering**
Of bad rebirths is the fruit of wrong-doing.
Therefore, even at the cost of your life,
Never do wrong—
This is the practice of Bodhisattvas.

Bad rebirths are those as a hell-being, hungry ghost or animal. Two of these we can't see at present, but people of many cultures, not just Buddhists, believe in different kinds of spirit-beings. In the hells the suffering of heat and cold is agonizing, and the thirty-two kinds of hungry ghosts continually experience hunger and thirst. Animals are all around us. There are those that live in the depths and those on the surface of the earth. They suffer from stupidity and confusion, are exploited by human beings and eaten alive by other animals. From where does all this suffering come? It doesn't arise causelessly, nor from discordant causes and is not thrust upon them by some external power. It is the result of past negative actions.

Even we, who are in a so-called good rebirth, constantly experience suffering. Whether we're high or low in society, ordained or lay, young or old, all of us experience mental and physical problems day in, day out. We must recognize that only our own past actions and not other living beings or circumstances are responsible.

Contemplating this will help us to develop conviction in the unfailing connection that exists between actions and their effects. Bodhisattvas, therefore, avoid wrong-doing even at the cost of their life. Happy days start once we take steps to purify past negative actions and refrain from creating new ones. When we meditate, we should evoke past suffering and ask ourselves what gave rise to it. We should also remember past happiness and consider how none of these experiences were uncaused or came from discordant causes. If we want happiness, we must create its causes, and if we don't want suffering, we must avoid the actions which give rise to it.

Our suffering is the fruition of past negative actions, but we also carry imprints of actions which have not yet borne fruit. Even if we do not succeed in completely eradicating their seeds, by applying the four counteractions[34] we can prevent them from ever bearing fruit. In the practices of the initial level, emphasis is placed on avoiding and purifying unwholesome actions which yield suffering and creating wholesome ones which bring happiness, so that a good rebirth may be attained. Practices of the intermediate level are intended to eradicate the disturbing emotions which lie at the root of all actions precipitating cyclic existence. The practices of a person of great capacity focus on getting rid even of the predispositions for disturbing emotions.

Although others' well-being is at the heart of all Buddhist practice, as a practitioner of the least capacity, we must first protect our own condition from deteriorating. This involves avoiding negative physical and verbal actions, for once we're in a bad rebirth, how can we help others? The practitioner of intermediate capacity understands that an unpeaceful, undisciplined mind is the root of cyclic existence, and that while we remain in cyclic existence, we cannot help others effectively. Concern for others prevents the practitioner of great capacity from being content with personal liberation. Such a person is motivated by a strong wish to help which is implemented through practice of the six perfections. The Buddha did not teach all this for self-aggrandizement but to show us how to live, develop spiritually and gain happiness. There's no need for blind faith in his words—we're free to investigate whether what he taught is valid.

This concludes the practices of the initial level which consist of recognizing the preciousness of our human life and its instability. We begin to think about future lives and the two possible kinds of rebirth which lie ahead. Motivated by concern for a good rebirth, we take heartfelt refuge and act out of a conviction in the connection between actions and their effects.

9 Like dew on the tip of a blade of grass, pleasures of the three worlds
Last only a while and then vanish.
Aspire to the never-changing
Supreme state of liberation—
This is the practice of Bodhisattvas.

Animals, nagas, humans and celestial beings all enjoy many different pleasures. In the form and formless realms coarse sensations of pleasure and coarse discrimination have stopped and neutral feelings are experienced as well-being. These pleasures and the domains in which they're experienced act as causes for craving and conceptions of a self. What appears as pleasure and is thought of as such is not real pleasure because of its association with cyclic existence. In the *Ornament for Mahayana Sutras* Maitreya says that excrement can never smell good (except perhaps to pigs!).

The pleasures experienced in good rebirths are the outcome of contaminated virtue and inevitably involve change and deterioration. They're unstable, untrustworthy and obviously not true pleasure, for when prolonged or intensified they lead to pain. There is no real happiness in such experiences, which are merely the alleviation of an intense form of suffering and the beginning of new suffering. If this were not so, how could what initially seems pleasurable become painful? For instance, if we feel cold and move close to the fire, the heat is pleasurable initially, but soon it becomes uncomfortable and then unbearable. At first we think something is great and later it makes us want to vomit! Since the pleasures of cyclic existence are evanescent like dew on the grass, which soon disappears when the sun shines on it, we should direct our attention to attaining liberation, the highest form of peace and lasting happiness.

We're told that everything we enjoy seeing and experiencing doesn't bring true happiness and that we should focus on gaining the lasting happiness of liberation. This advice is hard to follow when we've never tasted anything but ordinary happiness. Do we really believe any other kind exists?

The wish to free ourselves from all states within cyclic existence is the motivation, liberation is our object and the three kinds of training are the means to achieve it. Describing and contemplating the disadvantages of cyclic existence are not intended to depress us but to give us the impetus to seek freedom. We'll not do so unless we see cyclic existence as a troubled and oppressive condition. When we fully recognize our own suffering and want to free ourselves, it will be easy to empathize with others. Such empathy leads to compassion that wishes to alleviate their suffering and love that wishes them happiness, both of which are the basis for the altruistic intention.

6 Wish-fulfilling Jewels

10 **When your mothers, who've loved you since time without beginning,**
Are suffering, what use is your own happiness?
Therefore to free limitless living beings
Develop the altruistic intention—
This is the practice of Bodhisattvas.

Cyclic existence is beginningless and our rebirths, too, are without beginning. Therefore all living beings in the six realms of existence have been our fathers, mothers, sisters, brothers and beloved friends and, as such, have shown us loving care and kindness. What's happening to them? They're tormented by the suffering of cyclic existence in general and of the three bad states of rebirth in particular. When we see how much they suffer with our own eyes, what kind of people are we, if we turn our back and are concerned only with our own peace and happiness? It's like a mother leaving her only child, a little baby, lying out on the hot sand, while she enjoys a picnic under a shady tree. We must help and look after these suffering beings.

Buddhas first develop the altruistic intention to attain enlightenment in order to free living beings and bring them happiness. Then, to accomplish this, they train themselves in the six perfections. The closer we feel to living beings, the more we wish to help them overcome their suffering, which seems unbearable. This impels us to accept personal responsibility to rid them of it and bring them happiness. We then make the commitment to achieve enlightenment in order to carry out our resolve.

11 All suffering comes from the wish for your own happiness.
Perfect Buddhas are born from the thought to help others.
Therefore exchange your own happiness
For the suffering of others—
This is the practice of Bodhisattvas.

Another approach to developing the altruistic intention is the practice of equalizing and exchanging self and others.[35] All the past, present and future suffering in the three realms of existence comes from our compulsive desire for happiness and our misconception of the self. The thought "I" is ever-present, even in our dreams. We cling to the self and are concerned for its happiness, but happiness doesn't come of its own accord, so we grasp at everything we consider a means of insuring it. We're attached to our bodies and senses through which we hope to experience pleasure. We crave friends, possessions and places which we hope will make us happy. We try to acquire them but face frustration as we fail to get what we want and get much that we don't want. All this entails suffering now and in the future as well, since we perform many negative actions in our pursuit of happiness.

Buddhas, whose exclusive concern is others' well-being, are the source of good rebirths and liberation. As Bodhisattvas they developed the altruistic intention which grew out of their love and compassion. We, too, can do this. When we recognize that living beings are like wish-fulfilling jewels that grant us all temporary and ultimate happiness, we'll try to avoid harming them and help them as much as we can. Once we really understand the faults of selfishness and the great benefits of cherishing others, we'll begin to put others first instead of ourselves and readily undergo whatever hardships are necessary for their sake.

The meditation of giving and taking is done to develop the willingness to alleviate others' suffering and bring them happiness. When practising this, we begin by taking away the suffering and only then give happiness because normally it's impossible to enjoy anything while one is in pain. Traditionally, we include within our focus all sentient beings from those in the hell realms to Bodhisattvas on the tenth stage, taking away everything unpleasant which afflicts or limits them and harms their environment.

Having aroused a strong feeling of compassion wanting to free them from suffering, we start with those in the hot hells, taking on the anguish caused by heat and fire. It leaves through their right nostrils and comes towards us as a black ray which enters our left nostril. It doesn't just vanish into our body or elsewhere but strikes and decimates the selfishness massed at our heart.

Similarly, we take away the suffering of those in the cold hells, of hungry ghosts, animals and all the different forms of human suffering of which the principal are birth, aging, sickness and death. We take on the suffering of the demi-gods, who constantly experience jealousy, and of other celestial beings, who feel distraught when they approach death and realize they must take a less fortunate rebirth.

Although the aim is to include all living beings, as beginners, to make the practice more immediate, we may choose to concentrate on one group at a time. We can, for instance, imagine taking on the suffering of those in the area where we live. We may confine ourselves to human beings who are physically or mentally ill or those in a particular country where there is war or famine. To begin with whatever stimulates intense compassion in us is best. The practice may also be directed specifically towards humans and non-humans who harm us. We need to develop enough courage to take on every shred of their suffering and its causes and give away all our happiness.

If we're suffering from a particular disease or problem, we can imagine taking on the suffering of others in a similar situation, while making prayers that our suffering may replace theirs. When doing this, we visualize the black ray striking and destroying our sickness and then feel a sense of relief and satisfaction. If at first we find taking on others' suffering too daunting, we should start by accepting our own future suffering—the suffering we may experience later in the day, later in the year or later in this life.

We imagine giving our body, possessions and positive energy as a way of increasing our capacity to love. When giving away our body, we transform it into whatever is needed by living creatures and the environment throughout all realms of existence. Giving begins with a stream of white light which leaves our right nostril. For those in the hot hells, for instance, our body turns into rain which extinguishes the blazing fires and brings coolness. We also give them our body in the form of a precious human life with which to practise, as celestial mansions in which to live, as food and clothing and as spiritual teachers to instruct them, so that they can attain liberation and enlightenment. This is how we practise fulfilling all their temporary and ultimate needs.

Like the practice of taking, giving too can be performed in more specific contexts. We must employ whatever techniques are most effective to combat our narrow self-concern. We shouldn't feel frightened of giving and taking because they cannot harm us in any way. The practice is intended to build up courage and willingness to dedicate ourselves to others' well-being. It helps us to cherish others instead of just cherishing ourselves and to forget about ourselves instead of forgetting about them. At first it's hard to arouse real feeling but without discouragement we should at least repeat words that express our wish to give happiness and take on suffering. When we're familiar with the practice, we take on the suffering as we breathe in and give happiness as we breathe out. One day we may actually become able to do so. This is a very potent practice, and since mind and breath are closely connected, doing it will increase our love and compassion.

7 Transforming Trouble

When the five kinds of degeneration[36] abound, as they do at present, and practitioners who are just beginners face many obstacles and dangers, we must learn to turn adverse circumstances into conditions which support our spiritual path. Sutra describes extensively how this may be done, but in our text the method is summarized in the next ten verses.

12 **Even if someone out of strong desire**
Steals all your wealth or has it stolen,
Dedicate to him your body, possessions
And your virtue, past, present and future—
This is the practice of Bodhisattvas.

The first situation described is theft. A human or non-human being, under the influence of greed and strong craving, which blind him to the negativity of theft, steals or arranges to have our property stolen. How do we feel? Probably both furious and miserable. But we could try to stay calm instead of getting angry, upset or unhappy. Actually, compassion is appropriate when we think about this person's wrong-doing and the turbulent emotions which dominate him. Remembering that he's been a kind parent to us in numerous past lives, we try to arouse love for him. There are many others like him, all of whom we've vowed to free from suffering and lead across the ocean of cyclic existence. Remembering the promise we've made, it's a Bodhisattva's practice to dedicate everything to their well-being.

If we prepare our mind, we'll be ready when trying situations arise. Of course, it's totally contrary to convention to offer someone who has stolen from you everything else you possess. But the theft has been committed, and all we can do is bang our fist on the table in frustration. Getting angry, upset or trying to take revenge will not help to restore what we've lost. Instead we can use the opportunity to create positive energy.

13 Even if someone tries to cut off your head
When you haven't done the slightest thing wrong,
Out of compassion take all his misdeeds
Upon yourself—
This is the practice of Bodhisattvas.

The second situation that can be transformed from a hindrance into a conducive circumstance is when others harm us. Sometimes they do it in return for something we've done to them, but in this case the injury is inflicted without the slightest provocation. No matter how grave the harm, we shouldn't retaliate. We're already suffering, and our revenge cannnot stop the harm that's been done but will merely cause us additional suffering in future. It's a Bodhisattva's practice to wish that the other may be freed from the imprints of the negative action they've performed. Thinking in this way, we practise the meditation of taking on suffering and pray that all future negative consequences of the other's action will ripen on us. Arousing love and compassion by recognizing how the other person is out of control and governed by disturbing emotions will make us more able to deal with the situation.

We may also think that if we hadn't created a negative action in the past, we wouldn't have presented a target for harm. This entails taking responsibility for our own past actions. We should make a heartfelt prayer that other negative actions we've performed may also now ripen and come to an end.

Since we face constant obstacles and situations in which we experience harm, it's to our advantage not to let them overwhelm us but to regard them as an adornment. We really have no alternative! Does an angry response improve or exacerbate our situation? We can't say it would be bad to do what Togmay Sangpo suggests, but we may feel incapable. Nevertheless, if we think about and try out the extraordinary methods which this great Bodhisattva advocates, we may find that we're able to put his advice into practice and pass it on to others.

14 Even if someone broadcasts all kinds of unpleasant remarks
About you throughout the three thousand worlds,
In return, with a loving mind,
Speak of his good qualities—
This is the practice of Bodhisattvas.

The third situation has to do with unpleasant things said about us. Never mind the three thousand worlds, how would we feel if someone said unpleasant things about us on the BBC World Service or on Voice of America? Without getting angry or upset, could we with love and compassion for them speak of their accomplishments? Under such circumstances, it's difficult even to admit to oneself that the other person has any good qualities.

15 Though someone may deride and speak bad words
About you in a public gathering,
Looking on him as a spiritual teacher,
Bow to him with respect—
This is the practice of Bodhisattvas.

In the fourth situation, faults which we would prefer to keep hidden are made public in a gathering of friends, enemies and strangers. All our mistakes and weaknesses are enumerated. We've been humiliated in front of everybody. Normally we like to be praised in front of as many people as possible, but if we must face criticism, we prefer to do so in private. Still, we should treat the person who makes our faults known as a spiritual friend showing us the road to enlightenment. If we're genuinely trying to practise, we must recognize our faults and limitations and treat them as we would a sickness, applying the cure which will lead to inner health and strength.

It's a good spiritual teacher's responsibility to point out our faults and instruct us on how to deal with them. Only by recognizing them can we get rid of them. When others point out our faults, we should think whether their criticism is true or not. If it's justified, we should take note and make changes. If it's not, we should see the experience of being criticized as the outcome of our own past negative actions. This is how we can turn difficult circumstances to our own advantage and profit from them.

By making a radical transformation in our responses to such situations, we become true practitioners, but our external appearance and general behaviour should continue to be in keeping with our own culture. By not drawing attention to ourselves, we will encounter fewer obstacles. We can let the light of our love and compassion shine, but our accomplishments shouldn't be flaunted. Let them be like a light in a clay pot!

16 Even if a person for whom you've cared
Like your own child regards you as an enemy,
Cherish him specially, like a mother
Does her child who is stricken by sickness—
This is the practice of Bodhisattvas.

The fifth situation is when someone for whom we've cared with love and affection responds ungratefully and turns against us. Instead of feeling angry, the constructive reponse is to show them extra love and compassion. A mother with a sick child who is delirious and physically violent doesn't feel angry but lovingly does what she can to insure her child's recovery. Particularly in the case of ingratitude, we must try to cultivate compassion. One of the precepts in Geshe Chekawa's *Seven Points for Training the Mind* is to behave with particular care towards certain people: our family, enemies, those to whom we take an instant dislike and those whom we've helped and who injure us in return. There are three situations in which people harm us. We may have harmed them in the past and they're taking revenge. We may have done nothing at all to provoke them and yet they harm us, in which case we feel affronted. The most difficult situation to bear is when we've gone out of our way to be kind and they harm us in return. If we can cope with this ingratitude, we'll be able to deal with whatever else comes our way. It's most important not to regret the help we've given because this will only undermine the positive energy we created.

17 **If an equal or inferior person**
Disparages you out of pride,
Place him, as you would your spiritual teacher,
With respect on the crown of your head—
This is the practice of Bodhisattvas.

In the sixth situation someone who is our equal or superior in looks, accomplishments, wealth, strength or status denigrates us out of pride. Their words should be regarded as the words of a spiritual teacher. There may be a grain of truth in what they say, and perhaps we have not even been aware that we possess this fault. If so we should be thankful to our critic for pointing it out. If there is no truth in the belittling remarks, we may feel quite justified in getting angry, but this is not a useful reaction. The disparagement should be seen as the outcome of our own past actions, and since their fruition in this way brings their momentum to an end, gratitude is the most appropriate response.

We have the ability and intelligence to view these situations in a constructive way and profit from them. By doing so we make ourselves invulnerable to harm. If we don't get upset, we cannot be diminished or humiliated by them. Even if someone tries to put us down, we don't have to stay down. The Kadampa masters tell us that blame is better than praise because, though it's unpleasant to hear, it gives us a chance to get rid of our faults, whereas praise easily makes us conceited. Then our arrogant words and actions quickly offend others.

18 Though you lack what you need and are constantly disparaged,
Afflicted by dangerous sickness and spirits,
Without discouragement take on the misdeeds
And the pain of all living beings—
This is the practice of Bodhisattvas.

In the seventh situation everything is in decline. We are beset by difficulties, have trouble finding even the basic necessities of life, others disparage us, we suffer from sickness and pain and spirits afflict us. When things are going wrong and our physical condition is poor, we must guard against feeling distressed and losing our mental balance and clarity. We may be tempted to turn to drugs or drink to escape our misery, but if we can remain steadfast, we'll be better able to resolve our situation. Many other living beings are experiencing similar difficulties as a result of their past actions, while others are creating actions which will come to fruition in such experiences. It is a Bodhisattva's practice to think, "May my suffering replace theirs." The people who contribute to our troubles should be seen as spiritual teachers helping us to develop greater patience, compassion, love, enthusiastic effort, kindness, perseverance, the wish to gain freedom and an understanding of impermanence.

If we use our intelligence and abilities, just listening to the news can act as a teaching and deepen our understanding. If we don't, it may simply fan the flames of prejudice or cause us suffering.

19 Though you become famous and many bow to you,
And you gain riches to equal Vaishravana's,
See that worldly fortune is without essence,

And be unconceited—
This is the practice of Bodhisattvas.

Vaishravana is the great king and protector on the northern side of Mt. Meru, the central mountain of the universe. He is a lord of fabulous wealth, depicted holding a mongoose which spits jewels. Many people can deal with difficulties but get over-excited or arrogant when things go well. The eighth situation is one where we have the fortune to belong to a good family of noble lineage, are young, beautiful and have many accomplishments or enjoy favourable conditions such as wealth, fame and a position of authority. It's easy to misuse good fortune, but we must understand that all such assets are contaminated, unstable and have no essence. Instead of being conceited about our wealth, we could use it to alleviate poverty, provide for the spiritual community, build hospitals, donate medicines and commission representations of enlightened body, speech and mind. Using it in these ways creates merit. In the third chapter of *Engaging in the Bodhisattva Deeds* Shantideva says:

> Through giving, all sorrow is transcended
> And I will reach the sorrowless state.
> As all must be given up at one time,
> Giving it to living beings is best.

Since ultimately, when death comes, we must let go of everything, we should dedicate what we have to living beings. We all want happiness and the best way to achieve it is through generosity.

20 **While the enemy of your own anger is unsubdued,**
Though you conquer external foes, they will only increase.
Therefore with the militia of love and compassion
Subdue your own mind—
This is the practice of Bodhisattvas.

The ninth situation involves our response to provocative circumstances. These arise again and again, so it makes sense to deal with them constructively. Our anger destroys the causes we create for good rebirths and liberation. If we retaliate when our life, property or reputation is threatened and harm or kill one person, we make many enemies. That person's family and friends will wage a vendetta against us and relentlessly seek an opportunity for revenge. However, if we succeed in subduing our own anger, we may well be able to diffuse others' and create an atmosphere conducive to conciliation.

The destruction of positive energy is an invisible effect of anger, but there are many visible effects. When this sickness afflicts us, we can enjoy no peace. First we become upset, our mind is disturbed and troubled, and as the fire of anger blazes, we start to sweat. We turn red in the face and wrinkles and frowns appear. We end up saying nasty things and perhaps even shaking our fist. No matter how good-looking we are or how fine our clothes and jewellery, no one finds us attractive when we're angry. We only need to look in a mirror to see why. Joy and happiness fly out of the window, and we can't sleep even on the softest bed.

Our anger disturbs others and deprives them of peace. It is destabilizing, and just as fish avoid turbulent water, people feel uncomfortable in our presence, no matter how liberal we are with gifts. For these reasons we must destroy the inner enemy of anger and the lust for revenge by cultivating compassion and the wish to help others.

Clinging attachment and anger are the roots of non-virtue. Since we experience these emotions most strongly in relation to living beings, their antidotes must also be cultivated in relation to them. The antidote to clinging attachment is non-attachment, while the antidotes to anger are patience, love and compassion.

Anger cannot be counteracted by suppressing it but only by strengthening love and compassion. A pious wish not to get angry isn't enough. Overcoming anger demands on-going effort. When we know what constitutes real love and compassion, we can take the first effective steps towards developing them, driving anger out of our heart and replacing it with kindness. Just knowing what to do cannot bring about this transformation.

If something which has only ever harmed us since time immemorial inhabits our heart, how can we hope to find peace and happiness? Imagine sharing an apartment with three people—one of them is hard and menacing, one of them seems friendly but is totally disloyal and the third spurs the other two on to cause mischief. How can we trust and live in peace with such companions? Anger, desire and ignorance are like this.

In the fifth chapter of *Engaging in the Bodhisattva Deeds* Shantideva says:

> Unruly living beings are like space.
> There's not enough time to overcome them.
> Overcoming these angry thoughts
> Is like defeating all our enemies.

The number of uncouth and unruly living beings is as limitless as space and there isn't enough time to subdue them all, so we must deal with the source of all our problems, our own anger. If we're calm and peaceful, most of our enemies will vanish. Whether we talk a lot or a little about it, our priority should be to get rid of anger! The practices of the initial and intermediate level are aimed at countering clinging attachment. Persons of great capacity are concerned primarily with overcoming anger, and since ignorance is the root of all disturbing emotions, sooner or later we must eliminate it too.

21 Sensual pleasures are like saltwater:
The more you indulge, the more thirst increases.
Abandon at once those things which breed
Clinging attachment—
This is the practice of Bodhisattvas.

Our craving for sensual pleasure is like saltwater. The more we indulge, the more we crave. If we're thirsty, saltwater won't slake our thirst but only makes us thirstier. The objects of the senses are not bad in themselves, but no matter how much we indulge our craving, we'll never find satisfaction. Why not get rid of the craving?

Our senses encounter an object we find attractive and immediately the latent desire for pleasure is awakened. As we experience the object, contaminated pleasure arises which leads to a craving for its continuation. For example, the eye sees an attractive form which acts as a focal condition stimulating desire. Do pleasure or pain accompany visual perception? If not, we would also have to assert that they don't accompany tactile or gustatory perception, but pleasure seems to be present when we eat something tasty or feel something soft. Is it possible to enjoy objects, which normally stimulate desire, without craving? We offer external and internal sense objects to the Three Jewels. It would be meaningless to do this if they didn't enjoy them. Do they enjoy them with or without craving? Our most intense craving arises for internal sense objects such as the appearance, sound, smell, taste and physical sensation of another human being.

In the sixth chapter of *Engaging in the Bodhisattva Deeds* Shantideva says:

> For instance, if a fire which consumes
> One house moves to another,
> It is right to throw out anything
> Like straw which could ignite.
>
> Likewise anything to which the mind
> Is attached ignites the fire of anger.
> Fearing our merit will be consumed,
> It should be discarded at once.

If a house is on fire and the fire is spreading, we need to clear away straw, wood or anything else which is highly flammable and could cause a conflagration that would consume our entire home and property. Similarly, one way to prevent desire and attachment is to avoid contact with the objects that stimulate it. If anything comes between us and what we desire or if the thing to which we're attached is harmed or threatened, we instantly feel angry. This destroys the positive energy we've created.

Another way is not to avoid the objects but to contemplate their unappealing aspects, because desire results from focusing only on their attractive side. The third way is to contemplate their lack of true existence, since desire and clinging are based on seeing them as very real and objectively existent. Whichever technique we employ, the aim is to prevent desire and attachment, since they bring many other problems. This concludes the verses which deal with the cultivation of the conventional altruistic intention and how to overcome animosity and clinging attachment in general.

8 Dreams and Rainbows

22 Whatever appears is your own mind.
Your mind from the start was free from fabricated extremes.
Understanding this, do not take to mind
[Inherent] signs of subject and object—
This is the practice of Bodhisattvas.

This verse explains how to cultivate the ultimate altruistic intention. Everything that appears to the senses and the mind, everything associated with cyclic existence and the state of peace, is not as it seems. Nothing has the objective existence it seems to have. All are mere appearances. The people and places we see in dream or the magical illusion of a beautiful woman appear real to the mind or to the eye through the presence of causes of deception. They appear as long as these causes persist. But are they real people or places and does the woman really exist? They merely appear to exist. Similarly, through imprints for the conception of true existence and through the force of habit, things appear and appear to be truly existent. Yet when we try to find them, nothing can be found. Just as the objects of our perceptions lack true existence, so do the perceiving mind and mental activities. These, like the perceived objects, are also mere appearances. Thus everything that exists is free from all elaborations of true existence and is naturally beyond sorrow.[37]

It is the practice of Bodhisattvas to cultivate meditative stabilization free from the five faults: laziness, forgetting the focal object of meditation, agitation and slackness of concentration, not applying antidotes to these faults when necessary and applying them when it is unnecessary. They cultivate this meditative stabilization on reality, the emptiness of true existence of all that is apprehended and of the apprehending mind.

This is the way we, too, should meditate. It's great to be interested in meditation, but we need to know how to meditate. Is it just a question of sitting up straight? In that case statues are meditating all the time!

On the level of mere appearances everything is functional and operates in an entirely satisfactory way, but if we're not satisfied with this and wish to pinpoint agents, actions and their effects, nothing can be found. Since things seem to exist objectively, they should be findable if they exist as they appear. Their unfindablility indicates their lack of true existence but not their non-existence.

When we're told that things are mere deceptive appearances, we shouldn't misinterpret it as license to act in any way we please. Of course, none of us would be so silly! Appearances are extremely powerful. You dream your house is on fire and you're surrounded by flames. You can't escape and feel terrified. You wake up soaked in sweat and screaming. What a relief! It was just a nightmare and none of it actually happened, but while it all seemed to be happening, you were in anguish.

During meditative equipoise we focus on the emptiness of the objects perceived and perceiving consciousness. Then, in the subsequent period, we use our understanding that everything lacks true existence to deal with craving for objects to which we feel attracted.

23 When you encounter attractive objects,
Though they seem beautiful
Like a rainbow in summer, don't regard them as real
And give up attachment—
This is the practice of Bodhisattvas.

We respond to sense stimuli with attraction or aversion. Attachment and craving are directed towards those objects which seem attractive. Such attachment results from an incorrect mental approach which exaggerates the object's desirability. It projects and fabricates something which is not there but appears to reside in the object. We then feel a sense of delight which seems like our very best friend. Ignorance which apprehends the object as inherently existent is operating at the same time. If the incorrect mental approach which distorts and the ignorance on which it is based can be stopped, desire will not arise.

When you encounter attractive objects, remember that they're like a rainbow after a summer shower. They seem gorgeous but have no real substance and lack true existence. Since they're false and not as they appear, they shouldn't be regarded as real. They only appear real to mistaken perception. In verse twenty-one we saw how contact with attractive sense objects triggers latent desire and how contaminated pleasure resulting from our experience of the object stimulates craving. Here we see the process at a more subtle level, revealing the underlying causes of desire. Since we reach out for something which has been projected and fabricated, we cannot possibly get what we desire. The result is frustration which quickly turns into anger.

24 All forms of suffering are like a child's death in a dream.
Holding illusory appearances to be true makes you weary.
Therefore when you meet with disagreeable circumstances,
See them as illusory—
This is the practice of Bodhisattvas.

This verse shows how to overcome hostility by overcoming the misconception of true existence. All the suffering we experience of not getting what we want in life and getting what we don't want is like an illusion. A young woman who longs for a child dreams that she gives birth. In her dream she feels overjoyed, but then the child dies and she's grief-stricken. Everything she dreamed is just an illusion. Our suffering is like this.

When we encounter what we find disagreeable, aversion and painful feelings arise. These lead to unhappiness. Anger feeds on this unhappiness and soon destroys our serenity. We express the anger physically or verbally, which harms us and others. Anything which is harmful is said to be non-virtuous because its fruit is suffering. Thus there is present suffering because of our initial response and future suffering as a result of our actions. Here again, the object which stimulated the response appears to be truly or objectively existent and we tacitly assent to this appearance. Thus ignorance is present along with the aversion and hostility which arise on account of our incorrect mental approach. All the steps in this process are themselves deceptive appearances.

Since we've been born as a result of contaminated actions underlain by disturbing emotions, we all share the same kinds of suffering. If we take the time and allow ourselves to think fully about birth, sickness, aging and death, we'll find it quite unbearable. We hate to hear that we've aged. The mere words offend us. Even when we can see our grey hair and wrinkles in the mirror, we still love to be told we haven't changed a bit. This shows how distressing we find the process of aging. Not getting what we want and encountering what we wish to avoid are the commonest forms of human suffering and woe.

Just as sleep causes the young woman to feel that the birth and death of the child in her dream are real, predispositions for seeing things as truly existent affect our awareness and make things seem to exist from their own side. Because of our mental habits we're not conscious of how the whole process by which we suffer comes from our inablility to perceive that things are merely deceptive appearances. We hold what we consider disagreeable to be real, respond with aversion and struggle to rid ourselves of it. In doing this we perform negative actions which bring us pain. How exhausting it all is!

While the young woman is not aware that she is dreaming, the events in her dream arouse strong emotions, but in the case of a lucid dream, she would be aware that the birth and death of her child were just part of a dream. This would dramatically change her reactions. When we encounter unwanted experiences, we must remind ourselves that they are mere deceptive appearances and have no objective existence in and of themselves.

Once we understand what the author is saying, we can investigate what it means in terms of our own experience and how it can be useful to us in daily life. When we've digested it, we can also use what we've understood to give good advice to others. These things may be practised by anyone and do not conflict with the principles of other faiths.

9 Training and Serving

Bodhisattvas willingly accept responsibility to help, choosing ways which suit the disposition, interests and capacities of others, which means they need expertise in many fields. As part of their conduct, they practise the six perfections and commit themselves to this way of life because of their wish to attain enlightenment for the sake of all living beings. We claim to want to emulate them, so our interest in the teachings should not stem from mere curiosity or a taste for amazing facts. We know plenty of those already, and there are plenty more to discover elsewhere. Hopefully, we are really interested in what will bring us and others happiness and have recognized that external factors are not its main source. Happiness comes from transforming how we think, feel and act.

25 **When those who want enlightenment must give even their body,**
There's no need to mention external things.
Therefore without hope for return or any fruition
Give generously—
This is the practice of Bodhisattvas.

If we intend to attain enlightenment for the sake of all living beings, we must be prepared to part even with our beloved body, our flesh and bones, which we cherish above all else. What need is there to mention other totally untrustworthy things like money, land and houses? This is frightening, isn't it? We cherish our body and possessions, cling to them and cannot bear to part with them. The thought of giving them away is definitely unappealing.

Parting with them is hard enough, but even more difficult is to do it only out of love and compassion, without hope for anything in return either in this or future lives. Such is the inconceivable generosity of Bodhisattvas. The practice of generosity with regard to our body, for instance, has four aspects. "Giving" refers to developing the willingness to give ourselves completely. "Safeguarding" means not sacrificing our body till we're able to do so with ease. "Purifying" involves making sure that our generosity is not tainted by any negative actions. "Increasing" refers to the creation of virtue and positive energy to insure that we will have one human life after another in future.

If we give in the hope of receiving something in return, it's no more than a business transaction. When we make a material gift, give protection or instruction and hope our efforts will be recognized and appreciated, we run the risk of disappointment. If we do something entirely for others' benefit and don't expect thanks, we won't feel disappointed and may be pleasantly surprised. If the other person has any manners, they'll thank us for what we've done. It's important to appreciate and wish to repay kindness, at least with a "thank you."

26 Without ethics you can't accomplish your own well-being,
So wanting to accomplish others' is laughable.
Therefore without worldly aspirations
Safeguard your ethical discipline—
This is the practice of Bodhisattvas.

Without pure conduct a good rebirth is impossible. It's absurd to claim that we wish to attain enlightenment for the sake of all living beings, if we can't be bothered to observe ethical discipline. Unethical conduct leads to bad rebirths in which we have no opportunity to make good use of formerly created virtue. It's the practice of Bodhisattvas to safeguard their ethical discipline and vows as they would the pupils of their eyes. Ethical discipline, too, must be observed without any expectation or hope for reward and should be supported by a strong wish to gain freedom from cyclic existence. It automatically brings its own reward of happiness and a clear conscience as well as good consequences in future. The effects of our ethical conduct are undermined if we hope to gain something through it. We should even be prepared to bear others' lack of gratitude for our efforts. It isn't enough to wish others well, we must act, but generous actions of giving gifts, instruction or protection are spoiled through unethical conduct.

27 To Bodhisattvas who want a wealth of virtue
Those who harm are like a precious treasure.
Therefore towards all cultivate patience
Without hostility—
This is the practice of Bodhisattvas.

Human and celestial prosperity and happiness as well as the lasting happiness of liberation are the result of virtuous actions. Even Bodhisattvas, who enjoy such well-being and practise patience, have enemies. Each time they encounter one of them, they respond as if they'd found a precious treasure. Imagine finding a hidden treasure under the floorboards of your house. You didn't even need to go out and look for it. What luck! No need to seek opportunities to create virtue—to Bodhisattvas enemies are a hidden source of a wealth of virtue, a chance to practise patience. They regard those who dislike them as indispensable for developing greater patience and protecting their rich store of virtue from destruction by anger.

We can only hone our patience in relation to those who wish us ill. They are our teachers and we should pay them as much respect as we do the excellent teachings. There are three kinds of patience: the patience of taking no account of harm or the person who inflicts it, the patience of willingly accepting hardships and the patience of gaining certainty with regard to the teachings.

When we've been harmed, instead of feeling upset about what has happened, we should regard it as a deceptive appearance and evidence of the infallible nature of dependent arising. When someone harms us, we feel hurt and unhappy, but it's a Bodhisattva's practice to view the person who has inflicted the harm, the harm itself and the suffering as conditions furthering the practice of patience. This is why Bodhisattvas show the same respect to those who harm them as they do to the teachings.

We can bear harm more easily without getting upset if we remember that those harming us are not in control of themselves but are carried away by disturbing emotions. Instead of wishing to retaliate, we will feel compassion. Even so, we still experience unhappiness and suffering. The second kind of patience consists of willingly accepting such unhappiness and suffering as an outcome of our own past actions and seeing the one who harms as helping the momentum of those negative actions to come to an end. The third kind of patience concerns gaining certainty regarding the nature of reality. When we discover the actual way in which everything exists and familiarize ourselves with it, we will not feel upset, even when difficult circumstances as high as a mountain pile up around us.

When food is set on the table, we don't know whether it's good unless we taste it. We can't find out by gulping it down. If we want to experience the taste, we must chew slowly and savour what we're eating. It's the same with the teachings. In the window of some Japanese restaurants there are plastic models of the food served inside. They look delicious but if one were to bite into them, they would just taste of plastic. So you can't tell, unless you taste!

We may create virtue through giving the teachings or making material gifts and practise non-violence by avoiding unwholesome actions and being patient when others respond to our kindness ungratefully. That's how we prevent anger from destroying the virtue we've created. However, this virtue can only be strengthened and increased through enthusiastic effort.

We're enthusiastic about all kinds of activities and quite prepared to make effort in all kinds of worldly enterprises, but enthusiastic effort in the context of Buddhist practice means a delight in virtue, in those activities which are wholesome and benefit us and others. True enthusiastic effort is continuous, energetic and joyful because we recognize the benefits of what we're doing. This prevents us from feeling drained and discouraged, even when what we do is physically tiring.

28 **Seeing even Hearers and Solitary Realizers, who accomplish**
Only their own good, strive as if to put out a fire on their head,
For the sake of all beings make enthusiastic effort,
The source of all good qualities—
This is the practice of Bodhisattvas.

Hearers and Solitary Realizers are only concerned with personal liberation and single-mindedly do everything in their power to purify negativity and create virtue in order to free themselves from the bonds of contaminated actions and disturbing emotions. They're as single-minded as someone whose hair has caught fire or someone who suddenly finds a snake in their lap! If they're prepared to make such effort when their aim is only personal well-being and liberation, shouldn't we—who want to help all living beings attain ultimate happiness and for this reason alone seek full enlightenment, the ultimate source of all good qualities—be prepared to make much greater effort?

Enthusiastic effort involves overcoming the three kinds of laziness: delaying, attachment to trivial activities and discouragement. To overcome the first we contemplate the preciousness and precariousness of our human life. To counteract the second we think about the meaningful and important things we're capable of doing, about the great benefits of spiritual practice and the disadvantages of getting caught up in trivial pursuits or in the pleasure of sleeping excessively, lazing about and endless conversation. We find many good reasons not to feel discouraged when we compare our situation to that of other living beings and, indeed, of many other human beings. As fortunate human beings we can accomplish anything on which we set our mind. With the armour of enthusiastic effort, we're prepared to persevere for as long as necessary, no matter how difficult the task.

We feel interested in liberation and enlightenment, but when we're told it may take aeons of effort, the prospect is less appealing. "Isn't there a short-cut?" we inquire. We hear the secret teachings hold a quicker method, but our reason for wanting this is that we're not prepared to make the sustained effort demanded of a Bodhisattva. Yet the secret path requires even greater determination and ability. The proper reason for entering it is our urgency to become enlightened in order to help others.

Many people do good in the world. If they refine their motivation and do what they do, not out of a sense of obligation but with joy, their positive actions will be even more potent. We're frequently called upon to care for someone sick. We may dread it or feel discouraged when the sickness is protracted. Instead, if we can see the patient as giving us an opportunity to create powerful virtue, if we can stay enthusiastic and act with compassion, our nursing becomes a major practice. It requires skill to recognize when our enthusiasm is beginning to flag and we need to rest. Taking a break before we're burnt out allows us to continue later with renewed strength. Such skillful management of our energy is most important.

Human happiness, to a great extent, depends on having adequate resources. The fruit of material generosity to others is the enjoyment of future wealth, but we wish to enjoy this as a human and not as an animal. Ethical conduct insures a good future rebirth. The presence of supportive companions in the future is the result of practising patience now. Our future ability to accomplish whatever we undertake results from present enthusiastic effort. None of us could deny that we want these things.

We may gain a good body and mind, the possessions and friends we seek and be capable of acting effectively, but if we're distracted and dominated by disturbing emotions, we'll misuse these assets. To make our mind stable enough to prevent this, we must practise concentration.

29 Understanding that disturbing emotions are destroyed
By special insight with calm abiding,
Cultivate concentration which surpasses
The four formless absorptions—
This is the practice of Bodhisattvas.

Living beings remain in cyclic existence because of their disturbing emotions and the ignorance which underlies them. As long as this is present, there is no hope of liberation, let alone enlightenment. Ignorance is removed by knowledge and, though there are many kinds regarding conventional matters, the most important in this context is the understanding of reality. We who are fortunate and endowed with the ability to attain liberation are defeated by two things: our bodies are overwhelmed by death and our minds by ignorance. Only the cultivation of special insight into reality based on meditative stabilization can rid us of this ignorance.

Many forms of stabilization exist, but we should aim to achieve the kind through which we can get rid of the disturbing emotions and their seeds. Of all the life-forms we know, only humans have the capacity to do this, but very few show any interest in it. A mere interest, though good in that it establishes imprints, is not sufficient, for we must actually work at training the mind.

Worldly states of meditative stabilization and deep absorption, such as the four which belong to the formless realm, known as "limitless space," "limitless consciousness," "nothingness" and the "peak of existence," and those of the form realm may sound very attractive when we hear or read about them, but they cannot take us beyond cyclic existence. No matter how long we remain absorbed, eventually we must descend and take a more ordinary birth again.

Just as ethical discipline is essential for a human rebirth, we need special insight into reality free from all fabrications, special insight into the emptiness of the mind itself, based on calm abiding, if we wish to liberate ourselves from cyclic existence. This is where we should direct our efforts.

30 Since the five perfections without wisdom
Cannot bring perfect enlightenment,
Along with skillful means cultivate the wisdom
Which does not conceive the three spheres [as real]—
This is the practice of Bodhisattvas.

Practice of the five perfections without the understanding of reality remains contaminated, and though it may yield boundless happiness, it doesn't lead to omniscience. Love and compassion without the understanding of reality cannot help us to escape from worldly existence. On the other hand, we may easily remain trapped in a state of personal peace if we have understood reality but lack enough love and compassion. It is therefore the practice of Bodhisattvas to combine the two—skillful means and wisdom. Which of us can say we don't want to possess knowledge, kindness and pure conduct? Our text is a manual of instruction on how to gain these qualities and become a fully developed human being.

10 Beware

When we have committed ourselves to doing good and have taken a vow as an expression of our commitment, we must know what conflicts with it. If we don't understand this clearly, we cannot prevent mistakes. Our intention is often kind-hearted and we think we're doing good, but everything goes wrong because we don't see clearly enough and cannot recognize our own mistakes.

31 If you don't examine your own errors,
You may look like a practitioner but not act as one.
Therefore, always examining your own errors,
Rid yourself of them—
This is the practice of Bodhisattvas.

Togmay Sangpo challenges us to acknowledge our own particular weaknesses honestly. If we're trying to practise either the Great or the Lesser Vehicle, we must know what its practice entails. If we don't, we may easily mistake that which is contrary to the teachings for a good and true path. Hearing, thinking and meditating can be misused to reinforce our own prejudices and are easily tainted by worldly expectations and hopes.

Our main task is to recognize our faults and mistaken attitudes and do what we can to uproot them. Many mistakes result from the incorrect mental approach which, when no rational examination is made, instinctively sees what is impermanent as enduring, what is painful as pleasurable, what is unclean as clean and what lacks intrinsic existence as truly and objectively existent. Disturbing emotions arise particularly through viewing the body in this way. Our confusion prevents us from realizing clearly what needs to be adopted and discarded. We may appear to be a practitioner but are, in fact, only deceiving ourselves. Worse still, others may place their confidence in us and we end up deceiving them too. We can discover our faults by examining our physical, verbal and mental behaviour and weed them out through constant mindfulness, mental alertness and the application of appropriate antidotes.

Togmay Sangpo's words are deceptively simple, but we need only look at his commentary[38] on Shantideva's *Engaging in the Bodhisattva Deeds* to see what a good scholar he was. Besides, only someone with a deep understanding and personal experience of the teachings could have written this text.

32 If through the influence of disturbing emotions
You point out the faults of another Bodhisattva,
You yourself are diminished, so don't mention the faults
Of those who have entered the Great Vehicle—
This is the practice of Bodhisattvas.

While we must be meticulous about recognizing and dealing with our own faults, we should not point out the faults of Mahayana practitioners and others, except when we're motivated by a genuine desire to help them or to protect the precious teaching from harm. We may be tempted to denigrate their views or behaviour out of envy, competitiveness or simply because they hold different views or favour a different style of conduct from our own. This diminishes us because we've let ourselves be overwhelmed by prejudice and disturbing emotions. Dromtön Gyelway Jungnay[39] said that we should avoid pointing out others' faults, unless we have a very good reason for doing so. Being a busybody is quite likely to get us into trouble anyway! Moreover, criticizing someone who is an excellent field for the accumulation of positive energy is non-virtuous and has negative consequences.

Practitioners of the Great Vehicle are Bodhisattvas who have dedicated themselves completely to the welfare of countless living beings. Criticism of them is therefore cited here as the gravest instance. Most of us, when we eat food or wear clothes, create a debt to the innumerable living beings who have enabled us to enjoy these things. Bodhisattvas can enjoy them without creating such a karmic debt because they're constantly intent on the welfare of all living creatures.

33 Reward and respect cause us to quarrel
And make hearing, thinking and meditation decline.
For this reason give up attachment to
The households of friends, relations and benefactors—
This is the practice of Bodhisattvas.

Attachment to food, clothing and material possessions of any kind as well as to homage, praise and service easily leads to conflict among practitioners and between them and others. Not receiving what we desire breeds rancour which disturbs and distracts the mind. As a result our conduct and attitudes are likely to deteriorate. Attachment to friends, relatives, benefactors who provide us with material necessities, and to people we meet in the course of spiritual or secular activities is unhelpful. We may be tempted to keep the relationships going for our own ends by frequenting their homes and gradually become more and more involved in worldly matters.

We should give up attachment but not affection for these people. Attachment is constricting and doesn't allow the other person freedom. Even attachment to inanimate things is disturbing. If we're attached to our cups or wine glasses, we get anxious and irritated when we hear someone else in our kitchen washing up carelessly. If we aren't attached to a cup, we don't mind if it gets broken.

34 **Harsh words disturb the minds of others**
And cause deterioration in a Bodhisattva's conduct.
Therefore give up harsh words
Which are unpleasant to others—
This is the practice of Bodhisattvas.

Bodhisattvas must avoid all actions which are naturally unwholesome, especially the use of harsh or abusive language and hurtful words which can slip out so easily. Weapons hurt the body but words hurt the heart. The most cutting remarks can be made with gentility and refinement, and many hurtful things are said inadvertently in the course of normal conversation. Hurtful speech conflicts with practice of the four ways of maturing others,[40] one of which is to speak in an appealing way.

Particularly for Bodhisattvas, who work with and for others, good communication skills and pleasant speech are essential. Careless and hurtful speech is unpleasant, acts as a provocation and incites anger, which may cause the other person to perform negative actions.

35 **Habitual disturbing emotions are hard to stop through counteractions.**
Armed with antidotes, the guards of mindfulness and mental alertness
Destroy disturbing emotions like attachment
At once, as soon as they arise—
This is the practice of Bodhisattvas.

We should not be on friendly terms with our disturbing emotions. Shantideva says it's preferable to be beheaded or burnt alive than to be under their influence. Geshe Bengüngyel[41] described how he was always at the ready with the short spear of mindfulness and mental alertness, guarding the door by which the disturbing emotions enter. "If they turn aggressive, I'm aggressive too, but if they relax, so do I!"

We must keep constant watch for them because once these emotions get going, it's difficult to interrupt their momentum. They're as hard to stop as a mountain torrent. If we get to know them well, we'll recognize them the moment they begin, but this demands constant vigilance. Counteracting them with the right antidotes is a mark of conscientiousness. If our physical, verbal and mental activities become wholesome, we'll have no cause for guilt or regret. This will bring us happiness now and in the future.

36 **In brief, whatever you are doing,**
Ask yourself "What's the state of my mind?"
With constant mindfulness and mental alertness
Accomplish others' good—
This is the practice of Bodhisattvas.

Teachings, specifically on the conduct of Bodhisattvas, and Mahayana texts in general, contain many instructions, the essence of which is clearly to understand what is wholesome and unwholesome, always to bear it in mind and to be fully aware of our actions. We must become familiar with our own emotional patterns and mental habits. It doesn't matter where we live or what work we do, for such examination can be carried out anywhere, at any time. Cyclic existence, the result of contaminated actions underlain by disturbing emotions, and nirvana, the state of freedom from suffering, are both the outcome of our mind. Whether actions are positive or negative is primarily determined by the underlying state of mind with which they're performed.

Conclusion

Each morning we should begin by examining our state of mind. Do we feel faith, kindness, compassion and love, or disturbing and negative emotions like anger, greed, clinging and envy, or are we depressed and listless? Once we see what's going on, we work at nurturing the postive states and discarding the negative ones. Atisha advised that in company we should watch what we do and say, while in private we should watch our thoughts.

Bodhisattvas aim to accomplish others' well-being but cultivate introspection of this kind as well as love and compassion. First they strengthen and enrich themselves with virtue and make sure they do not create faulty actions. It's laughable to think of helping others if we're not strong and capable of looking after ourselves. We must be able to take care of ourselves physically and spiritually. We're grown-up, but from another point of view we're "infantile ordinary beings," as is often said in Buddhist texts.

Small children like sweets and surprises, but the best gift our parents and teachers give us is to teach us to fend for ourselves and survive in the world. The great spiritual teachers and texts offer us instructions for spiritual survival. They teach us how to get rid of self-destructive physical, verbal and mental habits and replace them with constructive behaviour.

37 To remove the suffering of limitless beings,
Understanding the purity of the three spheres,
Dedicate the virtue from making such effort
To enlightenment—
This is the practice of Bodhisattvas.

What do we dedicate? Studying, understanding and, primarily, practising what is contained in this text, as well as our past, present and future practice of the teachings in general, are a source of positive energy. We dedicate the positive energy we ourselves have created as well as that created by other both ordinary and exalted beings. Vividly evoking their many good actions which help and bring joy to others, we rejoice in them.

How is the energy dedicated? The dedication is made with the understanding that the three spheres—the agent, action and what is acted upon—are mutually dependent and empty of all intrinsic existence. The agent is the one making the dedication. The action is that of dedicating the positive energy. What is acted upon is the positive energy itself. To whom is the energy dedicated? To limitless living beings. For what purpose? For their ultimate happiness, their full enlightenment.

Taking refuge, generating the altruistic intention and making the dedication are quintessential Mahayana practices. We often do these automatically without feeling anything or thinking about the words. We may look around while we recite the relevant verses and become serious and focused only when we begin the actual practice of a particular deity. This could be a sign either that refuge and the altruistic intention have become second-nature or that the words have lost all meaning for us!

Many obstacles had to be overcome to invite the great Indian master Atisha to Tibet. When he taught, he spoke so much about refuge and karma that he was nicknamed the

"Refuge Lama" or "Karma Lama," but he was delighted to discover this because he considered these basic practices of supreme importance. Although Lha Lama Jangchup Wö,[42] who endured many difficulties to bring him to Tibet, was a scholar himself, he requested Atisha to give a teaching which would benefit everyone. Atisha, who was a great master and capable of explaining the profoundest and most complex aspects of reality or tantric practice, was touched by the simplicity and altruism of this request and responded by writing the *Lamp for the Path to Enlightenment*,[43] at the beginning of which he speaks of Lha Lama as "My good disciple." Even today this text continues to benefit innumerable people, not only Tibetans.

Dedicating our positive energy to the unsurpassable happiness of all living beings makes it limitless and inexhaustible. By accompanying the dedication with the understanding that the three spheres are empty of inherent existence, the virtue created cannot be destroyed by anger. It thus becomes an inexhaustible and indestructible magic treasure of virtue.

> **For all who want to train on the Bodhisattva path,**
> **I have written *The Thirty-Seven Practices of Bodhisattvas,***
> **Following what has been said by the excellent ones**
> **On the meaning of the sutras, tantras and treatises.**

For whom was the text written? For all those who are genuinely interested in Mahayana practice. It is based upon and is a summary of the three categories of sutra teachings, the four classes of tantra, specific advice for Bodhisattvas and oral instructions of the great masters.

> **Though not poetically pleasing to scholars**
> **Owing to my poor intelligence and lack of learning,**
> **I've relied on the sutras and the words of the excellent,**
> **So I think these Bodhisattva practices are without error.**

Togmay Sangpo claims that he lacks intelligence and the eloquence of a great scholar, but nevertheless he feels confident that he has given a reliable account of the practices undertaken by Bodhisattvas because he has drawn on the Buddha's personal instructions as found in sutra and tantra and as explained in the commentaries. We're at liberty to examine whether what he has said is correct.

However, as the great deeds of Bodhisattvas
Are hard to fathom for one of my poor intelligence,
I beg the excellent to forgive all faults,
Such as contradictions and non sequiturs.

Although he's confident of his sources, the author admits it's possible that there may be some errors, since the practices of Bodhisattvas are very profound and extensive. We learn that generosity leads to future resources, ethical conduct to a good rebirth, patience to the enjoyment of good companions and an attractive appearance. This is due to the connection between actions and their effects, a complex matter of which only the enlightened have full knowledge. They alone can perceive the subtle virtue in the mindstreams of ordinary and exalted beings. The author apologizes to all those excellent beings, who see things as they are, for any mistakes he has inadvertently made, for inconsistencies, contradictions and non sequiturs.

Through the virtue from this may all living beings
Gain the ultimate and conventional altruistic intention
And thereby become like the Protector Chenrezig
Who dwells in neither extreme—not in the world nor in peace.

Togmay Sangpo has explained the activities of Bodhisattvas in a way which is easy to understand and shows how they may be practised. His presentation is at once comprehensive and concise. Now he dedicates the considerable merit created through this, as well as former merit, for the benefit of living beings as limitless as space.

There are two important activities—one at the beginning and one at the end. When we sit down to meditate or to study, and certainly at the beginning of each day, we must create a really kind-hearted motivation, if it's not already present. Then, throughout the day, we check from time to time to see whether we're behaving as intended. If not, we try to correct our thoughts, feelings and actions. At night before we go to bed, we review the day. If all went well, we rejoice and dedicate the merit we've created for the good of all living beings. This encourages us to do the same next day and helps us to feel tranquil and free from regret when night comes. If we've made mistakes, we acknowledge and purify them. Going to sleep with positive and kind-hearted thoughts makes the sleep which follows virtuous. The Mahayana instructions for dying are exactly the same. Accustoming ourselves to positive states of mind is of utmost importance because what is most familiar comes to mind automatically.

The author dedicates the positive energy so that all living beings may gain the two kinds of altruistic intention: the ultimate altruistic intention, which focuses on emptiness and is accompanied by the compassionate wish for enlightenment, and the conventional altruistic intention which focuses on complete enlightenment for the sake of all beings. These make living beings rich in skillful means and wisdom, through which they can free themselves from the perils of worldly existence and solitary peace. The dedication is made with the wish that all beings may attain the state of Chenrezig who is free from these two extremes. He is the protector of the three worlds, the friend and helper of living beings.

The disturbing emotions underlain by ignorance which distorts reality keep us in worldly existence. Only through the correct understanding that everything is empty of inherent existence, diametrically opposed to the way in which things are perceived by ignorance, can we gain freedom from cyclic existence. Development of the altruistic intention depends upon the presence of love and compassion. These two will only arise if we see all living beings as near, dear and lovable and think about their suffering and lack of happiness. To feel this way about them, we train ourselves to recognize them as our mothers, to remember their great kindness and to feel a sense of gratitude which makes us want to repay that kindness. These feelings are aroused by focusing on their past kindness to us.

Contemplating the many faults of selfishness and the great benefits of cherishing others, we discover how living beings are like wish-fulfilling jewels to us, like our spiritual teachers and meditational deities, for everything we desire comes about through them. Once we feel close to them, thinking about their suffering and lack of happiness will arouse love and compassion. The stronger the love and compassion, the stronger the altruistic intention. Our own enlightenment is viewed only as a vehicle for alleviating others' suffering and bringing them happiness. When that wish is in the marrow of our bones and constantly present in our heart, we'll never be tempted by a state of solitary peace.

> **This was written for his own and others' benefit by the monk Togmay, an exponent of scripture and reasoning, in a cave in Ngülchu Rinchen.**[44]

The author wrote this text in order to familiarize himself again and again with the practices of Bodhisattvas and to acquaint others with them. Since he found conviction in the teachings through his knowledge of scripture, through reasoning and through personal experience, we can trust his words.

Dedication

May any merit that results from this work act as a cause for the Buddha's teaching to remain a living source of spiritual nourishment and for those who embody, hold and transmit it to enjoy long and fruitful lives.

Notes

Abbreviation

P: *Tibetan Tripiṭaka* (Tokyo-Kyoto: Tibetan Tripitaka Research Foundation, 1956)

1. The teachings on discipline (*'dul ba'i sde snod*) mainly set forth the training in ethical discipline (*tshul khrims kyi bslab pa*) or conduct (*spyod pa*). Those on knowledge (*mngon pa'i sde snod*) primarily explain the training in wisdom (*shes rab kyi bslab pa*) or the view (*lta ba*), while those on sutra (*mdo sde'i sde snod*) principally explain the training in meditative stabilization (*ting nge 'dzin gyi bslab pa*) or meditation (*sgom pa*).

2. Asaṅga (Thogs med), an Indian Buddhist master who lived in the fourth century, was a trailblazer in establishing the Chittamātra (*Sems tsam*) system of tenets, although he himself is said to have held the Prāsaṅgika-Mādhyamika (*dBu ma thal 'gyur pa*) view. His *Compendium of Knowledge* (*Abhidarmasamuccaya, mNgon pa kun btus*, P5550, Vol.112) sets out the focal objects of the paths: the aggregates, constituents and elements, the four noble truths and the twelve links of dependent arising. An extensive explanation of mind and mental activities is included. It contains instruction on how to practise by controlling one's senses and through training in ethical discipline, concentration and wisdom as well as an explanation of the thirty-seven factors concordant with enlightenment. It concludes by explaining the results of these prac-

tices through which all faults are brought to an end and the highest wisdom is attained. These topics are presented mainly from a Chittamātrin standpoint.

3. *zang zing med pa'i sdug bsngal*

4. Ay Monastery (E dgon, also Bo dong e) in Tsang (gTsang) lies on the route from Phuntsok Ling (Phun tshogs gling) to Tashi Lhunpo (bKra shis lhun po). It was founded by Geway Shenyen Mudra Chenpo (dGe ba'i bshes gnyen Mudra chen po) in 1049 and was the residence of the great translator Pang Lotsawa (dPang lo tsa ba chen po Blo gros brtan pa, 1276-1342) and his nephew.

5. *OM MANI PADME HUNG* is the mantra of Avalokiteshvara, the embodiment of enlightened compassion. The mantra is primarily associated with the four-armed form which holds a string of crystal prayer beads and the stem of a lotus. There are many interpretations of this profound mantra. In Ngülchu Dharmabhadra's (dNgul chu Dharma bhadra, 1772-1851) *Heart Wealth of Bodhisattvas* (*rGyal sras snying nor*), a commentary on Geshe Chekawa's (dGe bshes mChad kha ba) *Seven Points for Training the Mind* (*Blo sbyong don bdun ma*), the following brief interpretation occurs: the syllable *OM* serves as an invocation. *MANI* means jewel and signifies skillful means, while *PADME* means lotus and signifies wisdom. *HUNG* is the seed syllable of enlightened mind. Avalokiteshvara combines perfected skillful means and wisdom. Thus the mantra can be interpreted as a request, "You who hold the jewel and the lotus, please look on me with compassion and bless me to become like you."

6. Rishis (*drang srong*), "those who have gone straight," are said to have taken a path of complete honesty, free from any physical, verbal or mental deceit and dissimulation. They are frequently practitioners of heightened concentration who possess extra-sensory perception and miraculous powers.

Consultation with several senior Tibetan physicians has not thrown light on the "rishis' sickness." However, Tibetan medicine recognizes four general catergories of disease: temporary minor ailments which resemble sicknesses (*ltar snang 'phral nad*), real sickness occurring during one's life (*yongs grub tshe nad*), imaginary or imputed sicknesses inflicted by spirits (*kun brtags gdon nad*) and those which are governed by other factors in the form of previous actions (*gzhan dbang sngon las*). The rishis' sickness may refer to diseases of the last category, which are not affected by treatment. Patients either recover from these of their own accord or their condition worsens and nothing can be done. Togmay Sangpo's attitude implies full acceptance of the outcome, whatever it may be, as a consequence of past actions.

7. The disturbing attitudes and emotions and their seeds (*nyon sgrib*) obstruct freedom from the suffering of cyclic existence. Their imprints (*shes grib*) obstruct simultaneous direct perception of conventional and ultimate reality, which is the mark of complete enlightenment.

8. Geshe Langritangpa (dGe bshes Glang ri thang pa, 1054-1123) was one of the great Kadampa masters who were the direct spiritual heirs of the Indian master Atisha. Geshe Langritangpa wrote the *Eight Verses for Training the Mind* (*Blo sbyong tshig brgyad ma*), which inspired a number of other texts in the mind training (*blo sbyong*) tradition.

9. Mention of pure lands (*dag zhing*) is found in Mahāyāna texts. They are described as places where conditions are in every way favourable to spiritual development. There one enjoys the inspiring company of spiritual teachers and supportive spiritual companions. The wish to be born in such a place is not for one's own personal comfort and well-being, but because it allows one to make fast progress towards enlightenment, sought exclusively for the sake of helping others. The main practice which leads to rebirth in a pure land is purification of the mind.

10. Gyelwa Gendün Drup (rGyal ba dGe 'dun grub pa, 1391-1475) was retrospectively declared the First Dalai Lama. He was a devoted disciple of Tsongkhapa (Tsong kha pa, 1357-1419) and in 1447 founded Tashi Lhunpo Monastery (bKra shis lhun po), which became the seat of the Panchen Lamas.

11. Geshe Chekawa (dGe bshes mChad kha ba, 1101-1175) was the author of *Seven Points for Training the Mind.* Inspired by Geshe Langritangpa's words from the *Eight Verses for Training the Mind,* "May I accept the loss and offer the victory to others," he travelled to central Tibet in search of their author to learn more about this practice. To his disappointment Geshe Langritangpa had already passed away, but he was able to receive teaching from Geshe Sharawa (dGe bshes Sha ra ba, 1070-1130), who also held the instructions. Since he is said to have spent much time in burial grounds (*mchad pa*) to remind himself of impermanence, he became known as Geshe Chekawa.

12. Longdöl Lama (Klong rdol bla ma Ngag dbang blo bzang, 1719-1795) cultivated Tara as his meditational deity and paid homage to her

at the beginning of his many erudite works. He had visions in which received advice from her.

13. Literally the title means "The Thirty-seven Practices of Conqueror Children" (*rGyal sras lag len so bdun*). Conquerors are enlightened beings who have gained victory over the four demonic forces of involuntary death, the contaminated body, the disturbing emotions and the demonic force known as the "son of the gods" which prevents one from overcoming the other three demonic forces. Buddhas are intent only on the happiness of living beings. Bodhisattvas, who have vowed to attain complete enlightenment for the sake of all living beings, are their children in that they are born from the speech or teaching of Buddhas.

14. The Sanskrit Avalokiteshvara, also Lokeshwara, is translated as Chenrezig (sPyan ras gzigs) in Tibetan. Iconographically Chenrezig, the embodiment of perfect compassion, is most often depicted in a four-armed and in a thousand-armed form. The latter has eleven heads: the top head is the red face of Amitabha Buddha in an emanation body form with a crown protrusion and no jewels. Below this is a fierce black face with fangs, glaring eyes and flaming tresses. Below this are three heads; the central one is red, that to its left is white and that to its right is green. Below these are three more heads which are, in the same order, green, red and white respectively. Below these are three more: white, green and red respectively. These nine heads all have peaceful eyes.

The first two hands touch at the heart with a hollow between them symbolizing the form and wisdom bodies of enlightened beings. The second right hand holds crystal prayer beads, representing skillful means. The third right hand is in the gesture of supreme giving. From it flows nectar alleviating the hunger and thirst of hungry ghosts. This gesture denotes the promise to bestow everything that is needed, including the common and powerful attainments. The fourth right hand holds a wheel which denotes the uninterrupted turning of the wheel of teaching for living beings.

The second left hand holds an unsullied lotus to show that Chenrezig is untainted by any trace of selfishness. It also represents wisdom. The third left hand holds a water pot to symbolize the washing away of all disturbing attitudes and emotions. The fourth holds a bow and arrow to show that by teaching living beings he will lead them to the path that combines skillful means and wisdom. The other nine hundred and ninety-two arms and hands symbolize his ability to emanate universal monarchs. The eyes in the palms of the hands represent the ability to emanate the thousand Buddhas of the fortunate era. All this is for the benefit of living beings.

15. The five aggregates (*phung po*) consist of forms, feelings, discriminations, compositional factors and consciousnesses. These categories include all phenomena which are the product of causes and conditions and which undergo change moment by moment. The twelve sources (*skye mched*) consist of the six faculties—eye, ear, nose, tongue, body and mind—and their objects—visible forms, sounds, smells, tastes, tactile sensations and mental objects. These are the conditions through which consciousness arises. The eighteen constituents (*khams*) are the six faculties, the six objects and the six kinds of consciousness which arise through them.

16. The Indian Buddhist master Nāgārjuna (Klu sgrub, first to second century) was the trailblazer who established the Mādhyamika system of philosophical tenets. His *Treatise on the Middle Way*, also known as *Fundamental Wisdom* (*Madhyamakaśāstra, dBu ma rtsa ba'i shes rab*, P5224, Vol.95) presents diverse lines of reasoning to establish the nature of reality as emptiness of inherent existence, in accordance with the Perfection of Wisdom sutras.

17. The false view of the transitory collection (*'jig tshogs la lta ba*) focuses on the "I" attributed to the aggregates and misconceives its mode of existence. The aggregates, which make up body and mind, are a collection which is transitory, since it is produced and disintegrates moment by moment.

18. The Indian Buddhist master Chandrakīrti (Zla ba grags pa) was the main spiritual son of Nāgārjuna, whose works on sutra and tantra he elucidated and propagated. He lived in the monastic university of Nālandā during the seventh century. At one time he was in charge of stores and created a sensation by milking a cow that had been painted on the wall. He supplied all the monks with milk from this and still had plenty to spare. He did it to cut through their conceptions of true existence and to demonstrate that the most amazing things are possible because of their dependently arising nature. His *Supplement to the Middle Way* (*Madhyamakāvatāra, dBu ma la 'jug pa*, P5261, P5262, Vol.98) is a commentary on the meaning of Nāgārjuna's *Treatise on the Middle Way*, which it explains and supplements. It deals with the ten Bodhisattva stages.

19. Compassion focusing on living beings (*sems can tsam la dmigs pa'i snying rje*) is simply great compassion for suffering living beings. Compassion focusing on phenomena (*chos la dmigs pa'i snying rje*) is compassion for all living beings supported by an understanding of their impermanence. Compassion focusing on the unobservable (*dmigs med la dmigs pa'i snying rje*) is compassion for all living beings accompanied by an understanding of their lack of true existence. In fact all three kinds of compassion take living beings as their focal object.

20. The three worlds usually refers to the desire, form and formless realms (*'dod khams, gzugs khams, gzugs med khams*). The desire realm includes hell-beings, hungry ghosts, animals, humans, demi-gods and certain celestial beings. There are seventeen abodes within the form realm, rebirth in which results from the practice of meditative stabilization. There are four abodes within the formless realm, in which one is born as a result of more subtle states of meditative stabilization and through viewing the form realm as a coarse state and the formless realm as subtle and preferable. All these states of rebirth are still within cyclic existence. The three worlds may also refer to the worlds beneath, on and above the ground.

21. *'phrin las*

22. The Indian master and Bodhisattva Shāntideva (Zhi ba lha) lived in the monastic university of Nālandā during the eighth century. To others he appeared quite unaccomplished, and they said he only knew three things: how to eat, sleep and defecate. In an attempt to humiliate him, he was designated to teach before a large gathering. To everyone's amazement he showed himself to be a very great master by teaching his guide to the Bodhisattva's way of life, *Engaging in the Bodhisattva Deeds* (*Bodhisattvacaryāvatāra, Byang chub sems dpa'i spyod pa la 'jug pa*, P5272, Vol.99) and by displaying miraculous feats. This verse comes from the first chapter.

23. The scriptural teachings (*lung gi bstan pa*) are scriptures belonging to any of the three categories—discipline, higher knowledge or sutra—which correctly explain what should be discarded and cultivated. One holds the scriptural teachings by hearing or teaching them. One can also be said to hold them if, having taken refuge, one recites *OM MANI PADME HUNG* even once.

24. The insight aspect of the teachings (*rtogs pa'i bstan pa*) is any aspect of the excellent teachings, based on taking refuge, which belongs to

the three kinds of training, in ethical discipline, concentration or wisdom, the subject matter of the three categories of teaching.

25. The five extremely grave actions (*mtshams med lnga*), which lead straight to a bad rebirth without any intervening (*mtshams med pa*) life, are killing one's mother, father, or a Foe Destroyer, causing schism within the spiritual community, and drawing blood from the body of a Buddha with the intention to harm. The five almost as grave actions (*nye ba'i mtshams med lnga*), which also lead straight to a bad rebirth, are incest with one's mother if she is a Foe Detroyer, murdering a Bodhisattva, murdering an exalted being of the Lesser Vehicle, stealing what belongs to the spiritual community and destroying a monastery or reliquary monument out of hatred.

26. A human life of freedom and fortune is as hard to find as it is for a blind turtle, living on the ocean floor, who only surfaces once every hundred years, to put its neck through a golden yoke floating on the ocean, carried hither and thither by the wind and waves. A life of freedom and fortune is also as rare as it is for a mustard seed to remain on the point of a needle when mustard seeds are poured on to it, or for peas thrown against a wall or upright mirror to stick to it.

27. The eight worldly concerns (*'jig rten chos brgyad*) are being pleased when we receive gifts, when things go well, when we hear what is agreeable and when we are praised, and being displeased when we don't receive gifts, when things go badly, when we hear what is disagreeable and when we're criticized. These concerns keep us preoccupied with the well-being of this life and prevent us from focusing on well-being in future lives.

28. A traditional chuba (*chu pa*) is a loose wraparound coat with sleeves for men and with or without sleeves for women. It is made of wool or sheepskin and is belted in such a way as to create an ample pouch in front which can accomodate all kinds of possessions, babies and even lap-dogs. The modern chuba worn by women is fitted and lacks this practical advantage.

29. Tsampa (*rtsam pa*) is parched grain flour. The most common kind used in Tibet is made from roasted barley. It is used as a staple and eaten in different ways. Tea and butter may be added to it in one's own small wooden bowl, the contents of which are then mixed and kneaded into neat walnut-sized balls. Grown-ups often knead these balls for small children (and foreigners!) who make a mess at first because they

find it hard to stop the powdery tsampa escaping from the bowl. The balls may be eaten on their own accompanied by butter tea, with dry cheese, dried meat or with cooked vegetables. Tsampa is also used for preparing a porridge and for making ritual offerings.

30. The three physical virtues consist of taking every opportunity to avoid killing, stealing and sexual misconduct. The four virtues of speech are consciously to refrain from lying, using harsh language, divisive speech and idle chatter. In the course of such restraint, we try to protect life, treat others' property with respect, abstain from sexual activity completely if we've vowed celibacy or act considerately and mindfully in sexual relations. We also attempt to be truthful, gentle, conciliatory and meaningful in our verbal communication.

31. The *Ornament for Mahāyāna Sutras* (*Mahāyānasūtralamkāra, Thegs pa chen po'i mdo sde'i rgyan*, P5521, Vol.108) describes the conduct of Bodhisattvas. Asaṅga received this teaching directly from Maitreya, to whom it is attributed. Ideal teachers are said to have the following ten qualities: They are (1) disciplined in that they practise restraint from harmful physical, verbal and mental activity and abide by the three kinds of vows; (2) calm because their practice of concentration counters distraction, thereby overcoming coarse disturbing emotions; (3) very peaceful because their practice of wisdom thoroughly pacifies disturbing attitudes; (4) rich in scriptural knowledge regarding the three categories of teaching. They have (5) wisdom understanding suchness, the final mode of existence; (6) knowledge exceeding the student's in those matters in which the student seeks guidance; (7) wisdom and skill in presenting the teachings and guiding others; (8) love and compassion as their motivation for teaching. They are (9) untiring in their effort to help students, and such effort is continual. They are (10) patient in teaching and guiding students and are able to bear their ingratitude.

32. The *Great Exposition of the Stages of the Path* (*Lam rim chen mo*, P6001, Vol.152) is the longest and most comprehensive of Tsongkhapa's presentations of the paths of insight which lead to enlightenment. Tsongkhapa (Tsong kha pa, 1357-1419), born in Amdo, was a great reformer, dedicated practitioner and prolific writer. He founded Ganden Monastery (dGa' ldan rnam par rgyal ba'i gling) in 1409, the first of the monastic universities of the new Kadampa (bKa' gdams gsar ma) or Gelugpa (dGe lugs pa) tradition.

33. Those who have made a formal commitment to take refuge in the Three Jewels for as long as they live observe certain precepts. The individual precepts concern what we should and should not do with regard to each of the Three Jewels. The precepts in relation to the Buddha are that we should not consider any other refuge or source of protection higher than the Buddha and should respect all images of the Buddha and enlightened beings, whether or not they are well made or made of precious materials.

The precepts in relation to the teachings are, as far as possible, not to harm other living beings and to respect all texts which contain instruction on what behaviour and attitudes to adopt and what to discard, since they are intended for our own and others' well-being.

The precepts in relation to the spiritual community are not to allow our physical, verbal or mental activity to be influenced by those who dislike and oppose the Buddha's teaching and to respect all members of the spiritual community, no matter which form of Buddhism they practise, regarding them as spiritual companions and fostering a relationship with them based on the teachings and by offering them material help.

The general precepts are to take refuge again and again, remembering the special qualities and distinguishing features of the Three Jewels; to offer the first and best part of food and drink and to make other offerings, remembering the kindness of the Three Jewels; to encourage others, who show an interest, to take refuge; to entrust ourselves to the Three Jewels in whatever activities we undertake; not to give up the Three Jewels even in joke or at the cost of our life; to take refuge three times each day and three times each night, remembering the benefits of doing so: (1) we become a Buddhist, (2) are a suitable basis for all vows, (3) formerly accumulated karmic obstructions come to an end, (4) extensive stores of positive energy are easily accumulated, (5) harm from humans and non-humans cannot affect us, (6) we won't take bad rebirths, (7) we'll accomplish all our wishes, and (8) we'll become enlightened quickly.

34. According to Mahāyāna teaching, no matter how negative an action is, we can cleanse and purify ourselves of it by sincerely applying the four counteractions (*gnyen po stobs bzhi*). These four consist of the power of regret for what we have done (*rnam pa bsun 'byin pa'i stobs*), the power of the resolve not to repeat it (*nyes pa las slar ldog pa'i stobs*), the power of the basis (*rten gyi tobs*) and the power of counteractive

behaviour (*gnyen po kun tu spyod pa'i stobs*). The power of the basis involves taking heartfelt refuge and generating the altruistic intention. It's called the power of the basis because negative actions are either performed in relation to the Three Jewels, the Buddhas, their teaching and the spiritual community, or in relation to other living beings. We use those towards whom our negative action was directed as a basis for its purification. By taking refuge in the Three Jewels we counteract unwholesome actions in relation to them, and by generating the altruistic intention we counteract those in relation to other living beings. Anything positive we do with the intention of countering previous negative actions is counteractive behaviour.

35. "Equalizing self and others" (*bdag gzhan mnyam pa*) means giving as much importance to others' concerns, to the alleviation of their difficulties and suffering and to their attainment of happiness, as we do to our own. "Exchanging self and others" (*bdag gzhan brje ba*) refers to a complete reversal of our present attitudes. Now, our personal concerns are always of overriding importance and those of others are secondary. When we're able to exchange self and others, their concerns assume prime importance and our own take second place.

36. There are five kinds of degeneration (*snyigs ma lnga*):

(1) Previously there was a time of fullness without killing, stealing, sexual misconduct and strife. A gradual deterioration then occurred. The era in which the Buddha Shākyamuni came to this world and in which we live today is referred to as a time of strife, in which war, famine, epidemics, droughts, floods and other calamities abound. These are degenerate times (*dus snyigs ma*).

(2) Those who were easy to teach and guide because of their maturity and receptivity have gained realizations and are on the way to or have already attained liberation. The majority of those alive now are degenerate beings (*sems can snyigs ma*) because they are obstinate, have bad habits and are difficult to guide.

(3) At one time living beings had extremely long lives but gradually the length of their life decreased. Now, because of their degenerated life-span (*tshe snyigs ma*), humans rarely live much beyond eighty years and untimely death is frequent.

(4) Disturbing emotions have degenerated (*nyon mongs snyigs ma*) in that they are more crass, violent and lead to extremely unwholesome physical, verbal and mental activities.

(5) Degenerate views (*lta ba snyigs ma*), which are harmful and misleading, are prevalent, while views such as the correct understanding

of reality and of the connection between actions and their effects are unpopular.

37. Natural nirvāṇa (*rang bzhin myang 'das*), the natural state beyond sorrow, refers to emptiness and the fact that everything from the outset has never had any true or intrinsic existence.

38. This work is called *Ocean of Good Explanations, A Commentary on "Engaging in the Bodhisattva Deeds"* (*Byang chub sems dpa'i spyod pa la 'jug pa'i 'grel pa legs par bshad pa'i rgya mtsho*).

39. Dromtön Gyelway Jungnay ('Brom ston rGyal ba'i 'byung gnas, 1004-1064), the main Tibetan disciple of the Indian master Atīsha, was a lay practitioner and held layperson's vows. He was the founder of the Kadampa tradition. Although these days in traditional Tibetan drama he is portrayed wearing brocade robes, he was in fact from nomad stock and is said to have worn a simple sheepskin chuba.

40. The four ways of maturing others (*bsdu ba'i dngos po bzhi*) are skillful means employed to gain others' trust and make them mentally mature and receptive to increasingly profound teaching. Since most ordinary people are attracted by material generosity, Bodhisattvas first give gifts and act generously towards those they intend to help, in order to establish a positive relationship. When a suitable opportunity arises they teach in an informal, interesting and pleasant way adapted to the other person's capacities and inclinations. They then encourage him or her to apply in practice what was explained. At the same time, they take care to validate the advice they've given through personal example.

41. Geshe Bengüngyel (dGe bshes 'Ban gung rgyal) was one of the Kadampa masters. He had been a thief and brigand earlier in his life. As a practitioner he used to chide himself if he noticed he was doing or thinking anything unwholesome. He would say, "There you go again, you old villain Bengüngyel, still at your old ways!" But when he had done or thought something good, he would use his religious name and say, "Congratulations Geshe Tsultrim Gyelwa, keep up the good work!"

42. Both Lha Lama Jangchup Wö (lHa bla ma Byang chub 'od) and his uncle Lha Lama Yeshi Wö (lHa bla ma Ye shes 'od, probably 959-1036) belonged to the royal dynasty of Purang-Guge. Yeshi Wö refused to be ransomed when he was taken prisoner by a hostile king and died in prison, having made Jangchup Wö promise to use the gold he had

collected for securing his uncle's release to invite the great Indian master Atīsha to Tibet.

43. *Lamp for the Path to Enlightenment* (*Bodhipathapradīpa, Byang chub lam gyi sgron ma*, P5343, Vol.103) is the forerunner of the subsequent "lam rim" literature, which explains the stages of the path to enlightenment with strong emphasis on practice. Atīsha (982-1054) was born into a royal family probably in what is now Bengal. Owing to his parents' opposition, he had difficulty disengaging himself from royal life, but eventually, after a number of attempts, succeeded and became ordained. He studied with a hundred and fifty-seven spiritual masters but was always very moved when he recalled Dharmakīrti of Suvarnadvīpa, the master of the Golden Isles. Atīsha made a perilous thirteen-month sea journey to Indonesia to study with this master, with whom he remained for twelve years and to whom he attributed his development of the altruistic intention. After his return to India he lived in the monastic university of Vikramashīla, from where he was invited to Tibet.

44. Ngülchu Rinchen (dNgul chu rin chen) refers to the area of Ngülchu Cho Dzong (Ngul chu chos rdzong), the place where Togmay Sangpo practised and taught in the Shay Valley (bShad), through which a western tributary of the Rungchu (Rung chu) flows.

Tibetan Names and Their Transliteration

Chaksa Bumdron	Chag za 'bum sgron
Chenrezig	sPyan ras gzigs
Dromtön Gyelway Jungnay	'Brom ston rGyal ba'i 'byung gnas
Geshe Bengüngyel	dGe bshes 'Ban gung rgyal 'Tshul khrims rgyal ba
Geshe Chekawa	dGe bshes mChad kha ba
Geshe Langritangpa	dGe bshes Glang ri thang pa
Geshe Sharawa	dGe bshes Sha ra ba
Gyelsay Togmay Sangpo	rGyal sras Thogs med bzang po
Gyelwa Gendün Drup	rGyal ba dGe 'dun grub pa
Künchok Sangpo	dKon mchog bzang po
Lha Lama Jangchup Wö	lHa bla ma Byang chub 'od
Lha Lama Yeshi Wö	lHa bla ma Ye shes 'od
Longdöl Lama	Klong rdol bla ma
Ngülchu Dharmabhadra	Ngul chu Dhar ma bha dra
Pel Yewa	dPal ye ba
Pelden Yeshe	dPal ldan ye shes
Sangpo Pel	bZang po dpal
Tösay Künchok Pel	sTod sras dKon mchog dpal
Tsongkhapa	Tsong kha pa

Tibetan Commentaries

Two commentaries by the Nyingmapa master Ngawang Tenzin Norbu (Ngag dbang bstan 'dzin nor bu, 1867-1940):

rGyal sras lag len gyi 'brel pa gzhung dang gdams ngag zung 'jug bdud rtsi'i bum bzang

rGyal ba'i sras kyi lag len so bdun thun du bcad nas nyam su len byed lhan thabs byang chub myur lam

rGyal ba'i sras kyi lag len sum cu so bdun ma'i mchan 'grel yid kyi mun sel by Jigmay Tsültrim Pelzang ('Jigs med tshul khrims dpal bzang)

rGyal sras thogs med kyi mdzad pa'i lag len so bdun ma 'grel pa dpal gyi sgron mas brgyan pa by Acharya Sempa Dorjee (Varanasi: Nyingmapa Students' Welfare Committee, 1988)

Tibetan Text

༄༅། །རྒྱལ་སྲས་ཐོགས་མེད་ཀྱིས་མཛད་པའི་
ལག་ལེན་སོ་བདུན་མ་
བཞུགས་སོ།།

༄༅། །ན་མོ་ལོ་ཀེ་ཤྭ་ར་ཡ།

གང་གི་ཆོས་ཀུན་འགྲོ་འོང་མེད་གཟིགས་ཀྱང་།
འགྲོ་བའི་དོན་ལ་གཅིག་ཏུ་བརྩོན་མཛད་པ།
བླ་མ་མཆོག་དང་སྤྱན་རས་གཟིགས་མགོན་ལ།
རྟག་ཏུ་སྒོ་གསུམ་གུས་པས་ཕྱག་འཚལ་ལོ།

ཕན་བདེའི་འབྱུང་གནས་རྫོགས་པའི་སངས་རྒྱས་རྣམས།
དམ་ཆོས་བསྒྲུབས་ལས་བྱུང་སྟེ་དེ་ཡང་ནི།
དེ་ཡི་ལག་ལེན་ཤེས་ལ་རག་ལས་པས།
རྒྱལ་སྲས་རྣམས་ཀྱི་ལག་ལེན་ཤེས་པར་བྱ།

དལ་འབྱོར་གྲུ་ཆེན་རྙེད་དཀའ་ཐོབ་དུས་འདིར།
བདག་གཞན་འཁོར་བའི་མཚོ་ལས་བསྒྲལ་བྱའི་ཕྱིར།
ཉིན་དང་མཚན་དུ་གཡེལ་བ་མེད་པར་ནི།
ཉན་སེམས་བསྒོམ་པ་རྒྱལ་སྲས་ལག་ལེན་ཡིན།

གཉེན་གྱི་ཕྱོགས་ལ་འདོད་ཆགས་ཆུ་ལྟར་གཡོ།
དགྲ་ཡི་ཕྱོགས་ལ་ཞེ་སྡང་མེ་ལྟར་འབར།
བླང་དོར་བརྗེད་པའི་གཏི་མུག་མུན་ནག་ཅན།
ཕ་ཡུལ་སྤོང་བ་རྒྱལ་སྲས་ལག་ལེན་ཡིན།

ཡུལ་ངན་སྤངས་པས་ཉོན་མོངས་རིམ་གྱིས་འགྲིབ།
རྣམ་གཡེང་མེད་པས་དགེ་སྦྱོར་ངང་གིས་འཕེལ།
རིག་པ་དྭངས་པས་ཆོས་ལ་ངེས་ཤེས་སྐྱེ།
དབེན་པ་བསྟེན་པ་རྒྱལ་སྲས་ལག་ལེན་ཡིན།

ཡུན་རིང་འགྲོགས་པའི་མཛའ་བཤེས་སོ་སོར་འབྲལ།
འབད་པས་བསྒྲུབས་པའི་ནོར་རྫས་ཤུལ་དུ་ལུས།
ལུས་ཀྱི་འགྲོན་ཁང་རྣམ་ཤེས་འགྲོན་པོས་བོར།
ཚེ་འདི་བློས་བཏང་རྒྱལ་སྲས་ལག་ལེན་ཡིན།

གང་དང་འགྲོགས་ན་དུག་གསུམ་འཕེལ་འགྱུར་ཞིང་།
ཐོས་བསམ་བསྒོམ་པའི་བྱ་བ་ཉམས་འགྱུར་ལ།
བྱམས་དང་སྙིང་རྗེ་མེད་པར་སྒྱུར་བྱེད་པའི།
གྲོགས་ངན་སྤོང་བ་རྒྱལ་སྲས་ལག་ལེན་ཡིན།

གང་ཞིག་བསྟེན་ན་ཉེས་པ་ཟད་འགྱུར་ཞིང་།
ཡོན་ཏན་ཡར་ངོའི་ཟླ་ལྟར་འཕེལ་འགྱུར་བའི།
བཤེས་གཉེན་དམ་པ་རང་གི་ལུས་བས་ཀྱང་།
གཅེས་པར་འཛིན་པ་རྒྱལ་སྲས་ལག་ལེན་ཡིན།

རང་ཡང་འཁོར་བའི་བཙོན་རར་བཅིང་བ་ཡི།
འཇིག་རྟེན་ལྷ་ཡིས་སུ་ཞིག་སྐྱོབ་པར་ནུས།
དེ་ཕྱིར་གང་ལ་སྐྱབས་ན་མི་བསླུ་བའི།
དཀོན་མཆོག་སྐྱབས་འགྲོ་རྒྱལ་སྲས་ལག་ལེན་ཡིན།

ཤིན་ཏུ་བཟོད་དཀའི་ངན་སོང་སྡུག་བསྔལ་རྣམས།
སྡིག་པའི་ལས་ཀྱི་འབྲས་བུར་ཐུབ་པས་གསུངས།
དེ་ཕྱིར་སྲོག་ལ་བབ་ཀྱང་སྡིག་པའི་ལས།
ནམ་ཡང་མི་བྱེད་རྒྱལ་སྲས་ལག་ལེན་ཡིན།

སྲིད་གསུམ་བདེ་བ་རྩྭ་རྩེའི་ཟིལ་བ་བཞིན།
ཡུད་ཙམ་ཞིག་གིས་འཇིག་པའི་ཆོས་ཅན་ཡིན།
ནམ་ཡང་མི་འགྱུར་ཐར་པའི་གོ་འཕང་མཆོག
དོན་དུ་གཉེར་བ་རྒྱལ་སྲས་ལག་ལེན་ཡིན།

ཐོག་མེད་དུས་ནས་བདག་ལ་བརྩེ་བ་ཅན།
མ་རྣམས་སྡུག་ན་རང་བདེས་ཅི་ཞིག་བྱ།
དེ་ཕྱིར་མཐའ་ཡས་སེམས་ཅན་བསྒྲལ་བྱའི་ཕྱིར།
བྱང་ཆུབ་སེམས་བསྐྱེད་རྒྱལ་སྲས་ལག་ལེན་ཡིན།

སྡུག་བསྔལ་མ་ལུས་བདག་བདེ་འདོད་ལས་བྱུང་།
རྫོགས་པའི་སངས་རྒྱས་གཞན་ཕན་སེམས་ལས་འཁྲུངས།
དེ་ཕྱིར་བདག་བདེ་གཞན་གྱི་སྡུག་བསྔལ་དག
ཡང་དག་བརྗེ་བ་རྒྱལ་སྲས་ལག་ལེན་ཡིན།

སུ་བདག་འདོད་ཆེན་དབང་གིས་བདག་གི་ནོར།
ཐམས་ཅད་འཕྲོག་གམ་འཕྲོག་ཏུ་འཇུག་ན་ཡང་།
ལུས་དང་ལོངས་སྤྱོད་དུས་གསུམ་དགེ་བ་རྣམས།
དེ་ལ་བསྔོ་བ་རྒྱལ་སྲས་ལག་ལེན་ཡིན།

བདག་ལ་ཉེས་པ་ཅུང་ཟད་མེད་བཞིན་དུ།
གང་དག་བདག་གི་མགོ་བོ་གཅོད་བྱེད་ནའང་།
སྙིང་རྗེའི་དབང་གིས་དེ་ཡི་སྡིག་པ་རྣམས།
བདག་ལ་ལེན་པ་རྒྱལ་སྲས་ལག་ལེན་ཡིན།

འགའ་ཞིག་བདག་ལ་མི་སྙན་སྣ་ཚོགས་པ།
སྟོང་གསུམ་ཁྱབ་པར་སྒྲོགས་པར་བྱེད་ན་ཡང་།
བྱམས་པའི་སེམས་ཀྱིས་སླར་ཡང་དེ་ཉིད་ཀྱི།
ཡོན་ཏན་བརྗོད་པ་རྒྱལ་སྲས་ལག་ལེན་ཡིན།

འགྲོ་མང་འདུས་པའི་དབུས་སུ་འགའ་ཞིག་གིས།
མཚང་ནས་བྲུས་ཤིང་ཚིག་ངན་སྨྲ་ན་ཡང་།
དེ་ལ་དགེ་བའི་བཤེས་ཀྱི་འདུ་ཤེས་ཀྱིས།
གུས་པར་འདུད་པ་རྒྱལ་སྲས་ལག་ལན་ཡིན།

བདག་གི་བུ་བཞིན་གཅེས་པར་བསྐྱངས་པའི་མིས།
བདག་ལ་དགྲ་བཞིན་བལྟ་བར་བྱེད་ན་ཡང་།
ནད་ཀྱིས་བཏབ་པའི་བུ་ལ་མ་བཞིན་དུ།
ལྷག་པར་བརྩེ་བ་རྒྱལ་སྲས་ལག་ལེན་ཡིན།

རང་དང་མཉམ་པའམ་དམན་པའི་སྐྱེ་བོ་ཡིས།
ང་རྒྱལ་དབང་གིས་བརྙས་ཐབས་བྱེད་ན་ཡང་།
བླ་མ་བཞིན་དུ་གུས་པས་བདག་ཉིད་ཀྱི།
སྤྱི་བོར་ལེན་པ་རྒྱལ་སྲས་ལག་ལེན་ཡིན།

འཚོ་བས་འཕོངས་ཤིང་རྟག་ཏུ་མི་ཡིས་བརྙས།
ཚབས་ཆེན་ནད་དང་གདོན་གྱིས་བཏབ་ཀྱང་སླར།
འགྲོ་ཀུན་སྡིག་སྡུག་བདག་ལ་ལེན་བྱེད་ཅིང་།
ཞུམ་པ་མེད་པ་རྒྱལ་སྲས་ལག་ལེན་ཡིན།

སྙན་པར་གྲགས་ཤིང་འགྲོ་མང་སྤྱི་བོས་བཏུད།
རྣམ་ཐོས་བུ་ཡི་ནོར་འདྲ་ཐོབ་གྱུར་ཀྱང་།
སྲིད་པའི་དཔལ་འབྱོར་སྙིང་པོ་མེད་གཟིགས་ནས།
ཁེངས་པ་མེད་པ་རྒྱལ་སྲས་ལག་ལེན་ཡིན།

རང་གི་ཞེ་སྡང་དགྲ་བོ་མ་ཐུལ་ན།
ཕྱི་རོལ་དགྲ་བོ་བཏུལ་ཞིང་འཕེལ་བར་འགྱུར།
དེ་ཕྱིར་བྱམས་དང་སྙིང་རྗེའི་དམག་དཔུང་གིས།
རང་རྒྱུད་འདུལ་བ་རྒྱལ་སྲས་ལག་ལེན་ཡིན།

འདོད་པའི་ཡོན་ཏན་ལན་ཚྭའི་ཆུ་དང་འདྲ།
ཇི་ཙམ་སྤྱད་ཅིང་སྲེད་པ་འཕེལ་བར་འགྱུར།
གང་ལ་ཞེན་ཆགས་སྐྱེ་བའི་དངོས་པོ་རྣམས།
འཕྲལ་ལ་སྤོང་བ་རྒྱལ་སྲས་ལག་ལེན་ཡིན།

ཇི་ལྟར་སྣང་བ་འདི་དག་རང་གི་སེམས།
སེམས་ཉིད་གདོད་ནས་སྤྲོས་པའི་མཐའ་དང་བྲལ།
དེ་ཉིད་ཤེས་ནས་གཟུང་འཛིན་མཚན་མ་རྣམས།
ཡིད་ལ་མི་བྱེད་རྒྱལ་སྲས་ལག་ལེན་ཡིན།

ཡིད་དུ་འོང་བའི་ཡུལ་དང་འཕྲད་པ་ན།
དབྱར་གྱི་དུས་ཀྱི་འཇའ་ཚོན་ཇི་བཞིན་དུ།
མཛེས་པར་སྣང་ཡང་བདེན་པར་མི་ལྟ་ཞིང་།
ཞེན་ཆགས་སྤོང་བ་རྒྱལ་སྲས་ལག་ལེན་ཡིན།

སྡུག་བསྔལ་སྣ་ཚོགས་རྨི་ལམ་བུ་ཤི་ལྟར།
འཁྲུལ་སྣང་བདེན་པར་གཟུང་བས་ཨ་ཐང་ཆད།
དེ་ཕྱིར་མི་མཐུན་རྐྱེན་དང་འཕྲད་པའི་ཚེ།
འཁྲུལ་པར་ལྟ་བ་རྒྱལ་སྲས་ལག་ལེན་ཡིན།

བྱང་ཆུབ་འདོད་པས་ལུས་ཀྱང་བཏང་དགོས་ན།
ཕྱི་རོལ་དངོས་པོ་རྣམས་ལ་སྨོས་ཅི་དགོས།
དེ་ཕྱིར་ལན་དང་རྣམ་སྨིན་མི་རེ་བའི།
སྦྱིན་པ་གཏོང་བ་རྒྱལ་སྲས་ལག་ལེན་ཡིན།

ཚུལ་ཁྲིམས་མེད་པར་རང་དོན་མི་འགྲུབ་ན།
གཞན་དོན་འགྲུབ་པར་འདོད་པ་གད་མོའི་གནས།
དེ་ཕྱིར་སྲིད་པའི་འདུན་པ་མེད་པ་ཡི།
ཚུལ་ཁྲིམས་བསྲུང་བ་རྒྱལ་སྲས་ལག་ལེན་ཡིན།

དགེ་བའི་ལོངས་སྤྱོད་འདོད་པའི་རྒྱལ་སྲས་ལ།
གནོད་བྱེད་ཐམས་ཅད་རིན་ཆེན་གཏེར་དང་མཚུངས།
དེ་ཕྱིར་ཀུན་ལ་ཞེ་འགྲས་མེད་པ་ཡི།
བཟོད་པ་སྒོམ་པ་རྒྱལ་སྲས་ལག་ལེན་ཡིན།

རང་དོན་འབའ་ཞིག་བསྒྲུབ་པའི་ཉན་རང་ཡང་།
མགོ་ལ་མེ་ཤོར་བཟློག་ལྟར་བརྩོན་མཐོང་ན།
འགྲོ་ཀུན་དོན་དུ་ཡོན་ཏན་འབྱུང་གནས་ཀྱི།
བརྩོན་འགྲུས་རྩོམ་པ་རྒྱལ་སྲས་ལག་ལེན་ཡིན།

ཞི་གནས་རབ་ཏུ་ལྡན་པའི་ལྷག་མཐོང་གིས།
ཉོན་མོངས་རྣམ་པར་འཇོམས་པར་ཤེས་བྱས་ནས།
གཟུགས་མེད་བཞི་ལས་ཡང་དག་འདས་པ་ཡི།
བསམ་གཏན་སྒོམ་པ་རྒྱལ་སྲས་ལག་ལེན་ཡིན།

ཤེས་རབ་མེད་ན་ཕ་རོལ་ཕྱིན་ལྔ་ཡིས།
རྫོགས་པའི་བྱང་ཆུབ་ཐོབ་པར་མི་ནུས་པས།
ཐབས་དང་ལྡན་ཞིང་འཁོར་གསུམ་མི་རྟོག་པའི།
ཤེས་རབ་སྒོམ་པ་རྒྱལ་སྲས་ལག་ལེན་ཡིན།

རང་གི་འཁྲུལ་པ་རང་གིས་མ་བརྟགས་ན།
ཆོས་པའི་གཟུགས་ཀྱིས་ཆོས་མིན་བྱེད་སྲིད་པས།
དེ་ཕྱིར་རྒྱུན་དུ་རང་གི་འཁྲུལ་པ་ལ།
བརྟགས་ནས་སྤོང་བ་རྒྱལ་སྲས་ལག་ལེན་ཡིན།

ཉོན་མོངས་དབང་གིས་རྒྱལ་སྲས་གཞན་དག་གི
ཉེས་པ་སྒྲོགས་ན་བདག་ཉིད་ཉམས་འགྱུར་བས།
ཐེག་པ་ཆེ་ལ་ཞུགས་པའི་གང་ཟག་གི
ཉེས་པ་མི་སྨྲ་རྒྱལ་སྲས་ལག་ལེན་ཡིན།

རྙེད་བཀུར་དབང་གིས་ཕན་ཚུན་རྩོད་འགྱུར་ཞིང་།
ཐོས་བསམ་སྒོམ་པའི་བྱ་བ་ཉམས་འགྱུར་བས།
མཛའ་བཤེས་ཁྱིམ་དང་སྦྱིན་བདག་ཁྱིམ་རྣམས་ལ།
ཆགས་པ་སྤོང་བ་རྒྱལ་སྲས་ལག་ལེན་ཡིན།

རྩུབ་མོའི་ཚིག་གིས་གཞན་སེམས་འཁྲུག་འགྱུར་ཞིང་།
རྒྱལ་བའི་སྲས་ཀྱི་སྤྱོད་ཚུལ་ཉམས་འགྱུར་བས།
དེ་ཕྱིར་གཞན་གྱི་ཡིད་དུ་མི་འོང་བའི།
ཚིག་རྩུབ་སྤོང་བ་རྒྱལ་སྲས་ལག་ལེན་ཡིན།

ཉོན་མོངས་གོམས་ན་གཉེན་པོས་བཟློག་དཀའ་བས།
དྲན་ཤེས་སྐྱེས་བུས་གཉེན་པོའི་མཚོན་བཟུང་ནས།
ཆགས་སོགས་ཉོན་མོངས་དང་པོ་སྐྱེས་མ་ཐག
འབུར་འཇོམས་བྱེད་པ་རྒྱལ་སྲས་ལག་ལེན་ཡིན།

མདོར་ན་གང་དུ་སྤྱོད་ལམ་ཅི་བྱེད་ཀྱང་།
རང་གི་སེམས་ཀྱི་གནས་སྐབས་ཅི་འདྲ་ཞེས།
རྒྱུན་དུ་དྲན་དང་ཤེས་བཞིན་ལྡན་པ་ཡིས།
གཞན་དོན་སྒྲུབ་པ་རྒྱལ་སྲས་ལག་ལེན་ཡིན།

དེ་ལྟར་བརྩོན་པས་བསྒྲུབ་པའི་དགེ་བ་རྣམས།
མཐའ་ཡས་འགྲོ་བའི་སྡུག་བསྔལ་བསལ་བའི་ཕྱིར།
འཁོར་གསུམ་རྣམ་པར་དག་པའི་ཤེས་རབ་ཀྱིས།
བྱང་ཆུབ་བསྔོ་བ་རྒྱལ་སྲས་ལག་ལེན་ཡིན།

མདོ་རྒྱུད་བསྟན་བཅོས་རྣམས་ལས་གསུངས་པའི་དོན།
དམ་པ་རྣམས་ཀྱི་གསུང་གི་རྗེས་འབྲངས་ནས།
རྒྱལ་སྲས་རྣམས་ཀྱི་ལག་ལེན་སུམ་ཅུ་བདུན།
རྒྱལ་སྲས་ལམ་ལ་སློབ་འདོད་དོན་དུ་བཀོད།

བློ་གྲོས་དམན་ཞིང་སྦྱངས་པ་ཆུང་བའི་ཕྱིར།
མཁས་པ་དགྱེས་པའི་སྡེབ་སྦྱོར་མ་མཆིས་ཏེ།
མདོ་དང་དམ་པའི་གསུང་ལ་བརྟེན་པའི་ཕྱིར།
རྒྱལ་སྲས་ལག་ལེན་འཁྲུལ་མེད་ལགས་པར་སེམས།

འོན་ཀྱང་རྒྱལ་སྲས་སྤྱོད་པ་རླབས་ཆེན་རྣམས།
བློ་དམན་བདག་འདྲས་གཏིང་དཔག་དཀའ་བའི་ཕྱིར།
འགལ་དང་མ་འབྲེལ་ལ་སོགས་ཉེས་པའི་ཚོགས།
དམ་པ་རྣམས་ཀྱིས་བཟོད་པར་མཛད་དུ་གསོལ།

དེ་ལས་བྱུང་བའི་དགེ་བས་འགྲོ་བ་ཀུན།
དོན་དམ་ཀུན་རྫོབ་བྱང་ཆུབ་སེམས་མཆོག་གིས།
སྲིད་དང་ཞི་བའི་མཐའ་ལ་མི་གནས་པའི།
སྤྱན་རས་གཟིགས་མགོན་དེ་དང་མཚུངས་པར་ཤོག།

ཅེས་པ་འདི་རང་གཞན་ལ་ཕན་པའི་དོན་དུ་ལུང་དང་རིགས་པ་སྨྲ་བའི་བཙུན་པ་ཐོགས་མེད་ཀྱིས་དངུལ་ཆུའི་རིན་ཆེན་ཕུག་ཏུ་སྦྱར་བའོ།།